OPPOSING
VIEWPOINTS®
SERIES

The Banking Crisis

Other Books of Related Interest:

Opposing Viewpoints Series

Corporate Social Responsibility

Debt

Federal Budget

At Issue Series

Do Tax Breaks Benefit the Economy?

Should the Federal Government Bail Out Private Industry?

Current Controversies Series

Capitalism

The U.S. Economy

"Congress shall make no law ... abridging the freedom of speech, or of the press."

First Amendment to the U.S. Constitution

The basic foundation of our democracy is the First Amendment guarantee of freedom of expression. The *Opposing Viewpoints* series is dedicated to the concept of this basic freedom and the idea that it is more important to practice it than to enshrine it.

OPPOSING
VIEWPOINTS®
SERIES

The Banking Crisis

Dedria Bryfonski, Book Editor

GREENHAVEN PRESS
A part of Gale, Cengage Learning

GALE
CENGAGE Learning™

Detroit • New York • San Francisco • New Haven, Conn • Waterville, Maine • London

GALE
CENGAGE Learning

Christine Nasso, *Publisher*
Elizabeth Des Chenes, *Managing Editor*

© 2010 Greenhaven Press, a part of Gale, Cengage Learning

Gale and Greenhaven Press are registered trademarks used herein under license.

For more information, contact:
Greenhaven Press
27500 Drake Rd.
Farmington Hills, MI 48331-3535
Or you can visit our Internet site at gale.cengage.com

Articles in Greenhaven Press anthologies are often edited for length to meet page require-ments. In addition, original titles of these works are changed to clearly present the main thesis and to explicitly indicate the author's opinion. Every effort is made to ensure that Greenhaven Press accurately reflects the original intent of the authors. Every effort has been made to trace the owners of copyrighted material.

Image copyright Kirsty Pargeter, 2010. Used under license from shutterstock.com

LIBRARY OF CONGRESS CATALOGING-IN-PUBLICATION DATA

The banking crisis / Dedria Bryfonski, book editor.
       p. cm. -- (Opposing viewpoints)
    Includes bibliographical references and index.
    ISBN 978-0-7377-4854-3 (hardcover) -- ISBN 978-0-7377-4855-0 (pbk.)
    1. Bank failures--United States--Juvenile literature. 2. Banks and banking--Government policy--United States--Juvenile literature. 3. Investments, Foreign--United States--Juvenile literature. I. Bryfonski, Dedria.
    HG1573.B356 2010
    332.10973--dc22

                                                                           2009049026

Printed in the United States of America
1 2 3 4 5 6 7 14 13 12 11 10

Contents

Why Consider Opposing Viewpoints?   **11**

Introduction   **14**

Chapter 1: What Caused the Banking Crisis?

Chapter Preface   **22**

1. The Banking Crisis Was Caused by Bankers'   **24**
   Greed and Government Complicity
   Simon Johnson

2. Misguided Government Policies, Not Bankers'   **37**
   Greed, Caused the Banking Crisis
   Lawrence H. White

3. The Banking Crisis Was Caused   **50**
   by a Lack of Regulation
   Nouriel Roubini

4. Deregulation Did Not Cause the Banking Crisis   **60**
   James L. Gattuso

5. Excessive Compensation Packages Contributed   **66**
   to the Banking Crisis
   Paul Volcker

6. Not All Banks Have Excessive Executive   **75**
   Compensation Packages
   Jamie Dimon

7. The Banking Crisis Was Caused   **80**
   by Excessive Debt
   Andy Singh

Periodical Bibliography   **87**

Chapter 2: Is the U.S. Banking System in Jeopardy?

Chapter Preface   **89**

(continuation)

1. The Economy Is Turning Around   **91**
Christina Romer, interviewed by David Gregory

2. The Economy Will Not Turn Around   **97**
Until Structural Flaws Are Fixed
Sandy B. Lewis and William D. Cohan

3. Bailouts Are Necessary to Restore   **106**
the Banking System
Barack Obama

4. Bailouts Are Bad for the Economy   **115**
Daniel Mitchell

5. Some Banks Are Too Big to Let Fail   **122**
Ben S. Bernanke

6. Big Banks Should Be Allowed to Fail   **130**
Thomas M. Hoenig

Periodical Bibliography   **139**

Chapter 3: How Should the U.S. Banking System Be Fixed?

Chapter Preface   **141**

1. Banks Should Be Nationalized   **143**
Joseph E. Stiglitz

2. Nationalizing Banks Will Not Work   **149**
William M. Isaac

3. More Regulation of Banking Is Needed   **153**
Christopher J. Dodd

4. Reinventing Regulation   **159**
Steven Pearlstein

5. If Banks Are Too Big to Fail,   **164**
Take an Ax to Them
David Pauly

6. Big Banks Should Not Be Broken Up   **168**
Tim Fernholz

7. Small Banks Can Help Solve the Banking Crisis   **176**
Phillip Longman and Ellen Seidman

8. Executive Compensation of Bankers
Needs to Be Fixed   **188**
Gene Sperling

9. Regulating Executive Compensation
Will Not Solve the Banking Problem   **197**
Floyd Norris

Periodical Bibliography   **204**

Chapter 4: What Role Did Foreign Investment Play in the U.S. Banking Crisis?

Chapter Preface   **206**

1. Foreign Tax Havens Contributed
to the Banking Crisis   **208**
Rachel Keeler

2. Foreign Tax Havens Did Not Contribute
to the Banking Crisis   **218**
Richard W. Rahn

3. China Contributed to the Banking Crisis   **224**
Eswar Prasad

4. China Did Not Cause the Banking Crisis   **230**
Huang Xin

Periodical Bibliography   **234**

Glossary   **235**

For Further Discussion   **240**

Organizations to Contact   **243**

Bibliography of Books   **250**

Index   **254**

Why Consider Opposing Viewpoints?

> *"The only way in which a human being can make some approach to knowing the whole of a subject is by hearing what can be said about it by persons of every variety of opinion and studying all modes in which it can be looked at by every character of mind. No wise man ever acquired his wisdom in any mode but this."*
>
> John Stuart Mill

In our media-intensive culture it is not difficult to find differing opinions. Thousands of newspapers and magazines and dozens of radio and television talk shows resound with differing points of view. The difficulty lies in deciding which opinion to agree with and which "experts" seem the most credible. The more inundated we become with differing opinions and claims, the more essential it is to hone critical reading and thinking skills to evaluate these ideas. Opposing Viewpoints books address this problem directly by presenting stimulating debates that can be used to enhance and teach these skills. The varied opinions contained in each book examine many different aspects of a single issue. While examining these conveniently edited opposing views, readers can develop critical thinking skills such as the ability to compare and contrast authors' credibility, facts, argumentation styles, use of persuasive techniques, and other stylistic tools. In short, the Opposing Viewpoints Series is an ideal way to attain the higher-level thinking and reading skills so essential in a culture of diverse and contradictory opinions.

In addition to providing a tool for critical thinking, *Opposing Viewpoints* books challenge readers to question their own strongly held opinions and assumptions. Most people form their opinions on the basis of upbringing, peer pressure, and personal, cultural, or professional bias. By reading carefully balanced opposing views, readers must directly confront new ideas as well as the opinions of those with whom they disagree. This is not to simplistically argue that everyone who reads opposing views will—or should—change his or her opinion. Instead, the series enhances readers' understanding of their own views by encouraging confrontation with opposing ideas. Careful examination of others' views can lead to the readers' understanding of the logical inconsistencies in their own opinions, perspective on why they hold an opinion, and the consideration of the possibility that their opinion requires further evaluation.

Evaluating Other Opinions

To ensure that this type of examination occurs, *Opposing Viewpoints* books present all types of opinions. Prominent spokespeople on different sides of each issue as well as well-known professionals from many disciplines challenge the reader. An additional goal of the series is to provide a forum for other, less known, or even unpopular viewpoints. The opinion of an ordinary person who has had to make the decision to cut off life support from a terminally ill relative, for example, may be just as valuable and provide just as much insight as a medical ethicist's professional opinion. The editors have two additional purposes in including these less known views. One, the editors encourage readers to respect others' opinions—even when not enhanced by professional credibility. It is only by reading or listening to and objectively evaluating others' ideas that one can determine whether they are worthy of consideration. Two, the inclusion of such viewpoints encourages the important critical thinking skill of objectively evaluating an author's credentials and bias. This evaluation will illuminate an author's reasons for taking a particular stance on an issue and will aid in readers' evaluation of the author's ideas.

It is our hope that these books will give readers a deeper understanding of the issues debated and an appreciation of the complexity of even seemingly simple issues when good and honest people disagree. This awareness is particularly important in a democratic society such as ours in which people enter into public debate to determine the common good. Those with whom one disagrees should not be regarded as enemies but rather as people whose views deserve careful examination and may shed light on one's own.

Thomas Jefferson once said that "difference of opinion leads to inquiry, and inquiry to truth." Jefferson, a broadly educated man, argued that "if a nation expects to be ignorant and free . . . it expects what never was and never will be." As individuals and as a nation, it is imperative that we consider the opinions of others and examine them with skill and discernment. The *Opposing Viewpoints* series is intended to help readers achieve this goal.

David L. Bender and Bruno Leone,
Founders

Introduction

"The salient feature of the current financial crisis is that it was not caused by some external shock like OPEC raising the price of oil or a particular country or financial institution defaulting. The crisis was generated by the financial system itself."

—George Soros,
"The Crisis & What to Do About It,"
New York Review of Books,
December 4, 2008.

Although there are multiple opinions on the causes of the banking crisis, there is one thing on which there is general agreement. If banking were still practiced as it was by George Bailey in the movie *It's a Wonderful Life*, the crisis would not have happened.

To understand why the crisis occurred, it is useful to understand the chain of events that contributed to it and the role each played. This chain transformed the slightly stodgy, conservative banks of George Bailey's day to the high-stakes world of Wall Street, where large fortunes could be made with financial innovation.

The first step in the chain dates back to 1938, when the Federal National Mortgage Association (Fannie Mae) was established by the Franklin Delano Roosevelt administration to provide funds to banks so that they would be able to loan potential homeowners money to purchase their homes. The Federal Home Loan Mortgage Corporation (Freddie Mac) was created in 1970 to buy mortgages, repackage them, and sell them to investors. With the creation of these institutions, the concept of securitization was introduced, and the dynamics of banking changed dramatically. Prior to the 1970s, bankers knew their customers, and borrowing was a simple process. When people wanted to buy a house, they applied for a loan from their local bank. The loan stayed with the bank, and the buyer paid the bank back over a period of years. However, in the 1970s, there was a greater demand for housing than could be satisfied by the funds in community banks. The government told Fannie Mae and Freddie Mac to purchase mortgages from community banks, guaranteeing them against default, and to pool mortgages together to sell them to investors, who would be paid as the homeowners paid off their mortgages. A feature of this system of securitization that significantly contributed to the subprime mortgage crisis was that the entity granting the mortgage—the bank—had no financial incentive to make sure the borrower would not default.

In 1977 the Community Reinvestment Act was passed to address historic discrimination in lending practices. The act encouraged banks to lend to low- and moderate-income neighborhoods. While this was an admirable goal, some believe that to meet quotas established by this act, banks were forced to engage in imprudent lending. In the 1980s, coming off a recession, Congress enacted several laws designed to promote free enterprise by reducing regulations. One of these laws was the Alternative Mortgage Transaction Parity Act of 1982, an act that permitted the creation of adjustable rate mortgages, balloon mortgages, and negative amortization mortgages. These would be the types of mortgages that would create what became the subprime crisis, as buyers who did not qualify for standard mortgages, at prime interest rates, would be attracted to these higher-interest-rate mortgages and eventually default on them.

The Tax Reform Act of 1986 eliminated the tax deduction for interest paid on credit cards, but retained the deduction for interest on mortgages. This act made home equity loans highly attractive to many consumers. Believing that their homes would continue to rise in value, homeowners took out home equity loans to finance such purchases as cars and home improvement, increasing the amount of debt owed on their homes and leading to an unhealthy amount of personal debt in the financial system. In 1970, debt was 60 percent of domestic personal income. Debt increased to 134 percent of domestic personal income by mid-2008.

In 1999, Congress allowed commercial banks to operate as investment banks. This led to a wave of mergers and acquisitions in the financial industry, and greatly increased the size of a few institutions. Many believe that the more risk-prone behavior of investment banks came to dominate the culture of commercial banking, leading to banks taking on greater risks and higher debt. In 2008, when these supersized institutions teetered on the verge of collapse, their size and importance to the financial system posed a threat to the economy.

The Commodity Futures Modernization Act of 2000 excluded derivatives from regulation. Derivatives are financial instruments whose price is dependent upon one or more underlying assets, indexes, events, values, or conditions. The act created a boom in risky investments. As an example, credit default swaps, a popular derivative that provides insurance for securities in the event of a default, grew from a $1 trillion industry in 2002 to a $33 trillion business in 2009. These risky investments were not monitored by any agency. The fall of Wall Street stalwarts such as Bear Stearns, Lehmann Brothers, and American International Group (AIG) in 2008 were all directly attributable to the collapse of these unregulated financial instruments.

In 2001 a recession hit, prompted by the terrorist attacks of September 11. In an effort to bring the economy out of a recession, the Federal Reserve lowered its interest rate eleven times in 2001, beginning at 6.5 percent and ending at 1.75 percent. The rate would eventually go to 1 percent, where it would remain until 2004. William McChesney Martin, chairman of the Federal Reserve in the 1960s, said that is it the duty of the Fed "to take away the punch bowl [low interest rates] before the party really gets going." According to many economists, Alan Greenspan, chairman of the Federal Reserve from 1987 to 2006, failed to do this, instead further lowering interest rates. As a result, access to easy money fueled the housing boom.

With interest rates at an all-time low, the financial services industry was looking for attractive investment opportunities, and aggressively went after the real estate market. The availability of money also led to an increase in demand for home ownership among consumers. This was at a time when not a lot of houses were available, which led to an increase in prices. From the fourth quarter of 2002 to the fourth quarter of 2006, real estate prices rose by almost 32 percent. This created a greater demand for construction, with housing starts growing to over 2 million in 2005, more than 50 percent above the rate in the preceding years. In 2004, U.S. home ownership peaked at an all-time high of almost 70 percent.

During this time two fundamental shifts occurred in the housing market. Property purchase shifted from buying a place to live to making an investment, and lenders began offering loans to higher-risk buyers. In 2005, 40 percent of the home sales were for investment purposes or for second homes. The mortgage denial rate dropped to 14 percent in 2003 from 28 percent in 1997.

Much of the growth in the housing boom was in subprime mortgages. From 2003 to 2007, subprime mortgages quadrupled—from $332 billion to $1.3 trillion; in 2002 subprime mortgages were less than 9 percent of the market; in 2005 they were 25 percent of the market. At this point, there was significant money to be made by selling securitized mortgages, and the appetite for these encouraged lenders in the private sector to sell to those who would not have qualified before.

The financial institutions who bought these mortgages developed complex financial instruments that they believe reduced risk. They pooled mortgages into groups called tranches, then sold the group of mortgages to investors. The belief was that even if some of the mortgages defaulted, most in the pool would not default. They also sold mortgages in different classes—those with less risk would be paid off first, but the investors would get a lower return. The riskiest mortgages would be paid last, but would get the highest returns.

If all of this had been confined to the United States, it might have been self-limiting, as there was a finite sum of money available to be invested in these transactions. But a trade imbalance and the fact that nations such as China had far more household savings than the United States meant that there was a significant international appetite for these derivatives based on mortgages—many of them subprime. This lucrative market meant that bankers loosened their mortgage standards even more, to produce more product. This created the era of so-called NINJA loans (loans to people with *No Income, No Job*, and no *Assets*).

In 2004, the amount of debt in the financial system was increased when the federal Securities and Exchange Commission allowed banks to go from a ten-to-one leverage (the ratio of debt to asset) to as high as forty to one. This later became critical because as the housing market collapsed and housing prices decreased, more than a few banks realized they had bad assets on their books in the form of loans that would default and, with the amount of excessive debt they already had, no longer had assets to cover their liabilities.

Meanwhile, builders had overestimated the potential of the housing market. By 2006, there was a surplus of available houses, which resulted in prices being lowered. By the first quarter of 2007, the first year-over-year decline in nationwide housing prices since 1991 was recorded. Additionally, many buyers had adjustable-rate mortgages whose rates were increased, and they found they could not afford the higher payments. And because house prices were getting lower, instead of increasing, these homeowners could not get a new mortgage. Because many homeowners now owed more than their houses were worth, the number of foreclosures increased. The presence of foreclosures in the market lowers the overall value of houses, as foreclosed houses often sell for less than their appraised value. All of this meant that housing prices dropped 20 percent from mid-2006 to September 2008.

Subprime mortgages to those with poor credit histories were the most vulnerable in this environment, and the subprime mortgage industry collapsed, setting off shock waves throughout the financial system. Because subprime mortgages were a significant part of the complex financial investments that had been created, the institutions selling these investments also imploded. In June 2007, two Bear Stearns hedge funds that were invested in the U.S. housing market blew up, causing a panic in the financial market. By March 2008, the situation at Bear Stearns deteriorated to the point that it would be acquired by JPMorgan Chase at a price that essentially represented a fire sale.

In the third quarter of 2007, major investment banks such as Merrill Lynch—experiencing a collapse in its investments tied to the subprime mortgage market—began reporting large losses.

By 2008, there was concern that the threat to the financial system was not limited to the subprime mortgage market. Investors stopped investing, because it was generally not clear which investment instruments were exposed to bad mortgage debt. Additionally, banks already had taken on significant debt and were learning that many of their assets were toxic—that is, now devalued so much that they could not be sold. Their response was to simply stop lending money, creating a credit crisis.

In this environment, the most exposed institutions failed. In September 2008, Merrill Lynch was sold to the Bank of America, and Lehman Brothers collapsed. The U.S. government decided that certain institutions were "too big to fail"— their collapse would create a systemic catastrophe—and lent $85 billion to AIG in September 2008. In October 2008, in an effort to stabilize the economy, unfreeze credit markets, and prevent further erosion of confidence in the U.S. banking system, Congress authorized up to $700 billion to bail out banks.

In the viewpoints that follow, economists, politicians, analysts, and journalists offer varying opinions on the banking crisis in four chapters that ask What Caused the Banking Crisis? Is the U.S. Banking System in Jeopardy? How Should the U.S. Banking System Be Fixed? and What Role Did Foreign Investment Play in the U.S. Banking Crisis? The varying viewpoints in *Opposing Viewpoints: The Banking Crisis* help the reader get some idea of the complexity and difficulty of the current banking and economic crisis and what can be done to solve it.

OPPOSING
VIEWPOINTS®
SERIES

CHAPTER 1

What Caused the Banking Crisis?

Chapter Preface

Although many economists, politicians, and analysts lay the blame for the banking crisis on a specific target, most agree that there were multiple contributing factors. Indeed, the term "perfect storm" has been used in connection with the crisis by figures ranging from President Barack Obama to former U.S. secretary of the treasury Robert Rubin to Russian prime minister Vladimir Putin. Marc Simpson, associate professor of finance at Northern Illinois University's College of Business, makes the case that the causes of the financial crisis were the result of a variety of events and actions that lined up over the course of many years—even decades. "Taken alone, none of these events are necessarily bad, but you get a perfect storm when all of the events coincide and then you have a housing bubble that burst," Simpson says.

Others make the distinction that unlike a storm, which is an inevitable work of nature, the financial crisis was very much a work of man and could have been averted. Barry Ritholtz, a money manager and author of *Bailout Nation*, finds the perfect storm metaphor imperfect. "Rather, what led to the current situation," he asserts, "were numerous legislative, ideological, and business decisions that worked together to create a systemic failure."

What were some of the factors in this perfect, man-made financial storm? The following are some of the decisions, actions, and events most frequently cited:

- A period of deregulation, especially on the most complex financial instruments, that enabled bankers to create highly lucrative, highly complex financial instruments that concealed the level of risk inherent in them

- A greater number of subprime borrowers, created both by government policy and private sector self-interest

- The repeal of the Glass-Steagall Act in 1999 that allowed commercial banks to become more involved in the riskier business that formerly was only the business of investment banks.

- The lowering of interest rates by the Federal Reserve

- An influx of foreign money seeking investments in the U.S. housing market

- A housing boom that was created by easy-money policies and the loosening of underwriting standards

- A housing bust created when there was a glut of housing

- An incentive system in the finance industry that created a culture rewarding risk taking and short-term thinking

- The worldwide interconnectedness of the financial system, so that a failure in one part of it—namely, mortgages—created shock waves through the whole system

- The excessive debt that occurred in the banking system when in 2004 the Securities and Exchange Commission allowed big banks to borrow more heavily against their assets

- Credit rating agencies that gave questionable AAA ratings to investments that were comprised of significant amounts of subprime mortgages

- The erosion of confidence in the stability of U.S. banking that occurred due to the failure of such companies as Bear Stearns and Lehman Brothers

The authors in the following chapter present their viewpoints on the causes of the banking crisis.

> "Elite business interests . . . played a central role in creating the crisis, making ever-larger gambles, with the implicit backing of the government, until the inevitable collapse."

The Banking Crisis Was Caused by Bankers' Greed and Government Complicity

Simon Johnson

Simon Johnson is the Ronald A. Kurtz Professor of Entrepreneurship at the Massachusetts Institute of Technology's Sloan School of Management and a senior fellow at the Peterson Institute for International Economics in Washington, D.C. He is also a cofounder of BaselineScenario.com, a Web site on the global economy, and is a member of the Congressional Budget Office's Panel of Economic Advisers. From March 2007 through the end of August 2008, Johnson was the International Monetary Fund's chief economist and director of its research department.

Although multiple factors contributed to the financial crisis, the central cause, claims Johnson in the following viewpoint, is the overwhelming debt that banks incurred as the risky invest-

Simon Johnson, "The Quiet Coup: How Bankers Took Power, and How They're Impeding Recovery," *The Atlantic*, vol. 303, No. 4, May 2009, pp. 46–56. Reproduced by permission of the author.

ments they made defaulted. These risky investments were motivated by the potential for enormous profits and excessive compensation and were made possible by deregulatory policies. The relationship that existed between the financial industry and government gave government a misplaced confidence that bankers knew what they were doing—when in fact they did not, argues Johnson. He contends that the undue influence that Wall Street continues to have on the government is getting in the way of taking the harsh steps necessary to solve the crisis.

As you read, consider the following questions:

1. In the author's view, what are some of the similarities between the U.S. financial crisis and similar crises experienced by the markets of emerging nations such as South Korea and Russia?

2. What are some of the deregulatory policies that Johnson believes created an environment conducive to the financial crisis?

3. What are two problems that the author cites as blocking a solution to the crisis?

One thing you learn rather quickly when working at the International Monetary Fund [IMF] is that no one is ever very happy to see you. Typically, your "clients" come in only after private capital has abandoned them, after regional trading-bloc partners have been unable to throw a strong enough lifeline, after last-ditch attempts to borrow from powerful friends like China or the European Union have fallen through. You're never at the top of anyone's dance card.

The reason, of course, is that the IMF specializes in telling its clients what they don't want to hear. I should know; I pressed painful changes on many foreign officials during my time there as chief economist in 2007 and 2008. And I felt the effects of IMF pressure, at least indirectly, when I worked with governments in Eastern Europe as they struggled after 1989, and with the private sector in Asia and Latin America during the crises of the late 1990s and early 2000s. . . .

Becoming a Banana Republic

In its depth and suddenness, the U.S. economic and financial crisis is shockingly reminiscent of moments we have recently seen in emerging markets (and only in emerging markets): South Korea (1997), Malaysia (1998), Russia and Argentina (time and again). In each of those cases, global investors, afraid that the country or its financial sector wouldn't be able to pay off mountainous debt, suddenly stopped lending. And in each case, that fear became self-fulfilling, as banks that couldn't roll over their debt did, in fact, become unable to pay. This is precisely what drove Lehman Brothers into bankruptcy on September 15, [2008,] causing all sources of funding to the U.S. financial sector to dry up overnight. Just as in emerging-market crises, the weakness in the banking system has quickly rippled out into the rest of the economy, causing a severe economic contraction and hardship for millions of people.

But there's a deeper and more disturbing similarity: elite business interests—financiers, in the case of the U.S.—played a central role in creating the crisis, making ever-larger gambles, with the implicit backing of the government, until the inevitable collapse. More alarming, they are now using their influence to prevent precisely the sorts of reforms that are needed, and fast, to pull the economy out of its nosedive. The government seems helpless, or unwilling, to act against them.

Top investment bankers and government officials like to lay the blame for the current crisis on the lowering of U.S. interest rates after the dotcom bust or, even better—in a "buck stops somewhere else" sort of way—on the flow of savings out of China. Some on the right like to complain about Fannie Mae [the Federal National Mortgage Association] or Freddie Mac [the Federal Home Loan Mortgage Corporation], or even about longer-standing efforts to promote broader homeownership. And, of course, it is axiomatic to everyone that the regulators responsible for "safety and soundness" were fast asleep at the wheel.

But these various policies—lightweight regulation, cheap money, the unwritten Chinese-American economic alliance, the promotion of homeownership—had something in common. Even though some are traditionally associated with Democrats and some with Republicans, they *all* benefited the financial sector. Policy changes that might have forestalled the crisis but would have limited the financial sector's profits— such as Brooksley Born's[1] now-famous attempts to regulate credit-default swaps[2] at the Commodity Futures Trading Commission, in 1998—were ignored or swept aside.

The financial industry has not always enjoyed such favored treatment. But for the past 25 years or so, finance has boomed, becoming ever more powerful. The boom began with the [Ronald] Reagan years, and it only gained strength with the deregulatory policies of the [Bill] Clinton and George W. Bush administrations. Several other factors helped fuel the financial industry's ascent. Paul Volcker's monetary policy in the 1980s, and the increased volatility in interest rates that accompanied it, made bond trading much more lucrative. The invention of securitization[3] interest-rate swaps,[4] and credit-default swaps greatly increased the volume of transactions that bankers

1. Brooksley Born was chair of the Commodity Futures Trading Commission from 1996 to 1999. In her role, she warned of the risks inherent in some complex financial instruments but was ignored.
2. A credit default swap (CDS) is a transaction where the buyer of a bond or loan makes payments to the seller, who guarantees the creditworthiness of the product. The buyer receives a payment from the seller if the product goes into default.
3. Securitization is the process of aggregating similar types of investments, typically loans or mortgages, into a common pool, then selling that pool of investments.
4. An interest rate swap is a financial transaction often used by hedge funds in which one party exchanges a stream of interest payments for the other party's stream of cash flows.

could make money on. And an aging and increasingly wealthy population invested more and more money in securities[5], helped by the invention of the IRA [individual retirement account] and the 401(k) plan. Together, these developments vastly increased the profit opportunities in financial services.

Not surprisingly, Wall Street ran with these opportunities. From 1973 to 1985, the financial sector never earned more than 16 percent of domestic corporate profits. In 1986, that figure reached 19 percent. In the 1990s, it oscillated between 21 percent and 30 percent, higher than it had ever been in the postwar period. This decade [2000–2009], it reached 41 percent. Pay rose just as dramatically. From 1948 to 1982, average compensation in the financial sector ranged between 99 percent and 108 percent of the average for all domestic private industries. From 1983, it shot upward, reaching 181 percent in 2007.

The great wealth that the financial sector created and concentrated gave bankers enormous political weight—a weight not seen in the U.S. since the era of J.P. Morgan (the man)[late nineteenth and early twentieth centuries]. . . .

The Wall Street–Washington Corridor

The American financial industry gained political power by amassing a kind of cultural capital—a belief system. Once, perhaps, what was good for General Motors was good for the country. Over the past decade, the attitude took hold that what was good for Wall Street was good for the country. The banking-and-securities industry has become one of the top contributors to political campaigns, but at the peak of its influence, it did not have to buy favors the way, for example, the tobacco companies or military contractors might have to. Instead, it benefited from the fact that Washington insiders al-

5. A security is an investment instrument issued by a corporation, government, or other organization (excluding insurance policies and fixed annuities] that represents financial value. Securities can be debt [such as banknotes or bonds], equity [such as stocks], or derivative [such as futures, options, or swaps].

ready believed that large financial institutions and free-flowing capital markets were crucial to America's position in the world.

One channel of influence was, of course, the flow of individuals between Wall Street and Washington. . . .

Wall Street is a very seductive place, imbued with an air of power. Its executives truly believe that they control the levers that make the world go round. A civil servant from Washington invited into their conference rooms, even if just for a meeting, could be forgiven for falling under their sway. Throughout my time at the IMF, I was struck by the easy access of leading financiers to the highest U.S. government officials, and the interweaving of the two career tracks. . . .

Wall Street's seductive power extended even (or especially) to finance and economics professors, historically confined to the cramped offices of universities and the pursuit of Nobel Prizes. . . .

From this confluence of campaign finance, personal connections, and ideology there flowed, in just the past decade, a river of deregulatory[6] policies that is, in hindsight, astonishing:

- insistence on free movement of capital across borders;

- the repeal of Depression-era regulations separating commercial and investment banking;

- a congressional ban on the regulation of credit-default swaps;

- major increases in the amount of leverage[7] allowed to investment banks;

- a light (dare I say *invisible?*) hand at the Securities and Exchange Commission in its regulatory enforcement;

6. Deregulation is the removal or easing of government rules and regulations in the economic system.
7. Leverage is the use of debt to grow an investment.

- an international agreement to allow banks to measure their own riskiness;

- and an intentional failure to update regulations so as to keep up with the tremendous pace of financial innovation.

The mood that accompanied these measures in Washington seemed to swing between nonchalance and outright celebration: finance unleashed, it was thought, would continue to propel the economy to greater heights.

U.S. Oligarchs and the Crisis

The oligarchy[8] and the government policies that aided it did not alone cause the financial crisis that exploded [in 2008]. Many other factors contributed, including excessive borrowing by households and lax lending standards out on the fringes of the financial world. But major commercial and investment banks—and the hedge funds[9] that ran alongside them—were the big beneficiaries of the twin housing and equity-market bubbles of this decade, their profits fed by an ever-increasing volume of transactions founded on a relatively small base of actual physical assets. Each time a loan was sold, packaged, securitized, and resold, banks took their transaction fees, and the hedge funds buying those securities reaped ever-larger fees as their holdings grew.

Because everyone was getting richer, and the health of the national economy depended so heavily on growth in real estate and finance, no one in Washington had any incentive to question what was going on. Instead, Fed Chairman [Alan] Greenspan and President [George W.] Bush insisted metronomically that the economy was fundamentally sound and

8. An oligarchy is a system where power resides with a small, elite group of inside individuals and institutions who act together to control the system.
9. A hedge fund is a pooled private investment fund that seeks to maximize returns with strategies that include unconventional investments and investments that cannot quickly be converted to cash, such as real estate.

that the tremendous growth in complex securities and credit-default swaps was evidence of a healthy economy where risk was distributed safely. . . .

By now, the princes of the financial world have of course been stripped naked as leaders and strategists—at least in the eyes of most Americans. But as the months have rolled by, financial elites have continued to assume that their position as the economy's favored children is safe, despite the wreckage they have caused. . . .

Throughout the crisis, the government has taken extreme care not to upset the interests of the financial institutions, or to question the basic outlines of the system that got us here. In September 2008, [Treasury secretary] Henry Paulson asked Congress for $700 billion to buy toxic assets[10] from banks, with no strings attached and no judicial review of his purchase decisions. Many observers suspected that the purpose was to overpay for those assets and thereby take the problem off the banks' hands—indeed, that is the only way that buying toxic assets would have helped anything. Perhaps because there was no way to make such a blatant subsidy politically acceptable, that plan was shelved.

Instead, the money was used to recapitalize banks, buying shares in them on terms that were grossly favorable to the banks themselves. As the crisis has deepened and financial institutions have needed more help, the government has gotten more and more creative in figuring out ways to provide banks with subsidies that are too complex for the general public to understand. . . .

Even leaving aside fairness to taxpayers, the government's velvet-glove approach with the banks is deeply troubling, for one simple reason: it is inadequate to change the behavior of a financial sector accustomed to doing business on its own terms, at a time when that behavior *must* change. As an un-

---

10. A toxic asset is an economic resource whose value has dropped significantly or for which there is no longer a market.

named senior bank official said to the *New York Times* [in late 2008], "It doesn't matter how much Hank Paulson gives us, no one is going to lend a nickel until the economy turns." But there's the rub: the economy can't recover until the banks are healthy and willing to lend.

The Way out

Looking just at the financial crisis (and leaving aside some problems of the larger economy), we face at least two major, interrelated problems. The first is a desperately ill banking sector that threatens to choke off any incipient recovery that the fiscal stimulus might generate. The second is a political balance of power that gives the financial sector a veto over public policy, even as that sector loses popular support.

Big banks, it seems, have only gained political strength since the crisis began. And this is not surprising. With the financial system so fragile, the damage that a major bank failure could cause—Lehman was small relative to Citigroup or Bank of America—is much greater than it would be during ordinary times. The banks have been exploiting this fear as they wring favorable deals out of Washington. Bank of America obtained its second bailout package (in January [2009]) after warning the government that it might not be able to go through with the acquisition of Merrill Lynch, a prospect that [the Department of the] Treasury did not want to consider.

The challenges the United States faces are familiar territory to the people at the IMF. If you hid the name of the country and just showed them the numbers, there is no doubt what old IMF hands would say: nationalize troubled banks and break them up as necessary.

Nationalization[11] would not imply permanent state ownership. The IMF's advice would be, essentially: scale up the standard Federal Deposit Insurance Corporation [FDIC] process.

---

11. Nationalization is taking a private enterprise into the public ownership of a national government.

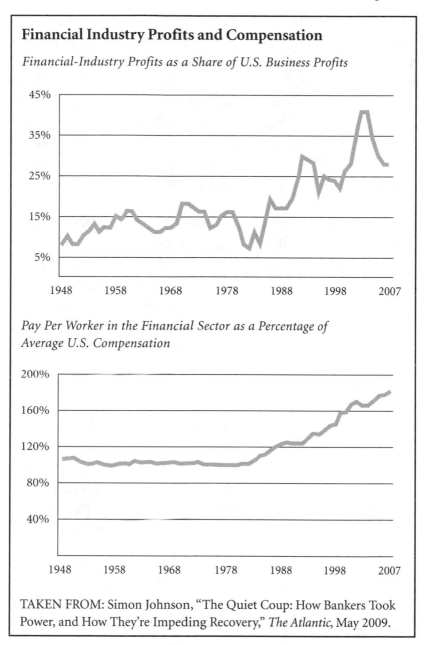

Financial Industry Profits and Compensation

Financial-Industry Profits as a Share of U.S. Business Profits

Pay Per Worker in the Financial Sector as a Percentage of Average U.S. Compensation

TAKEN FROM: Simon Johnson, "The Quiet Coup: How Bankers Took Power, and How They're Impeding Recovery," *The Atlantic*, May 2009.

An FDIC "intervention" is basically a government-managed bankruptcy procedure for banks. It would allow the government to wipe out bank shareholders, replace failed management, clean up the balance sheets, and then sell the banks back to the private sector. The main advantage is immediate recognition of the problem so that it can be solved before it grows worse. . . .

Cleaning up the megabanks will be complex. And it will be expensive for the taxpayer; according to the latest IMF numbers, the cleanup of the banking system would probably cost close to $1.5 trillion (or 10 percent of our GDP [gross domestic product]) in the long term. But only decisive government action—exposing the full extent of the financial rot and restoring some set of banks to publicly verifiable health—can cure the financial sector as a whole.

This may seem like strong medicine. But in fact, while necessary, it is insufficient. The second problem the U.S. faces—the power of the oligarchy—is just as important as the immediate crisis of lending. And the advice from the IMF on this front would again be simple: break the oligarchy. . . .

To ensure systematic bank breakup, and to prevent the eventual reemergence of dangerous behemoths, we also need to overhaul our antitrust legislation. Laws put in place more than 100 years ago to combat industrial monopolies were not designed to address the problem we now face. The problem in the financial sector today is not that a given firm might have enough market share to influence prices; it is that one firm or a small set of interconnected firms, by failing, can bring down the economy. The [Barack] Obama administration's fiscal stimulus evokes FDR [Franklin Delano Roosevelt, president during the Great Depression in the thirties], but what we need to imitate here is Teddy Roosevelt's trust-busting. . . .

Two Paths

To paraphrase Joseph Schumpeter, the early-20th-century economist, everyone has elites; the important thing is to change them from time to time. If the U.S. were just another country, coming to the IMF with hat in hand, I might be fairly optimistic about its future. Most of the emerging-market crises that I've mentioned ended relatively quickly, and gave way, for the most part, to relatively strong recoveries. But this, alas, brings us to the limit of the analogy between the U.S. and emerging markets.

Emerging-market countries have only a precarious hold on wealth, and are weaklings globally. When they get into trouble, they quite literally run out of money—or at least out of foreign currency, without which they cannot survive. They *must* make difficult decisions; ultimately, aggressive action is baked into the cake. But the U.S., of course, is the world's most powerful nation, rich beyond measure, and blessed with the exorbitant privilege of paying its foreign debts in its own currency, which it can print. As a result, it could very well stumble along for years—as Japan did during its lost decade [the 1990s]—never summoning the courage to do what it needs to do, and never really recovering. A clean break with the past—involving the takeover and cleanup of major banks—hardly looks like a sure thing right now. Certainly no one at the IMF can force it.

In my view, the U.S. faces two plausible scenarios. The first involves complicated bank-by-bank deals and a continual drumbeat of (repeated) bailouts, like the ones we saw in February [2009] with Citigroup and AIG. The administration will try to muddle through, and confusion will reign. . . .

Our future could be one in which continued tumult feeds the looting of the financial system, and we talk more and more about exactly how our oligarchs became bandits and how the economy just can't seem to get into gear.

The second scenario begins more bleakly, and might end that way too. But it does provide at least some hope that we'll be shaken out of our torpor. It goes like this: the global economy continues to deteriorate, the banking system in east-central Europe collapses, and—because eastern Europe's banks are mostly owned by western European banks—justifiable fears of government insolvency spread throughout the Continent. Creditors take further hits and confidence falls further. The Asian economies that export manufactured goods are devastated, and the commodity producers in Latin America and Africa are not much better off. A dramatic worsening of the global environment forces the U.S. economy, already staggering, down onto both knees. The baseline growth rates used in the administration's current budget are increasingly seen as unrealistic, and the rosy "stress scenario" that the U.S. Treasury is currently using to evaluate banks' balance sheets becomes a source of great embarrassment.

Under this kind of pressure, and faced with the prospect of a national and global collapse, minds may become more concentrated.

The conventional wisdom among the elite is still that the current slump "cannot be as bad as the Great Depression." This view is wrong. What we face now could, in fact, be worse than the Great Depression—because the world is now so much more interconnected and because the banking sector is now so big. We face a synchronized downturn in almost all countries, a weakening of confidence among individuals and firms, and major problems for government finances. If our leadership wakes up to the potential consequences, we may yet see dramatic action on the banking system and a breaking of the old elite. Let us hope it is not then too late.

> "The actual causes of our financial troubles were unusual monetary policy moves and novel federal regulatory interventions."

Misguided Government Policies, Not Bankers' Greed, Caused the Banking Crisis

Lawrence H. White

Lawrence H. White is the F.A. Hayek Professor of Economic History at the University of Missouri–St. Louis and an adjunct scholar at the Cato Institute, a think tank with strong libertarian leanings. He is the author of Competition and Currency, Free Banking in Britain, *and* The Theory of Monetary Institutions.

In the following viewpoint, White disputes the theories that greed and deregulation are responsible for the financial crisis. Government, rather than business, is culpable for the crisis, he claims. The two main government policies White finds respon-

sible are the cheap money policy following the 2001 recession, which set off the housing bubble, and actions of Congress and the Department of Housing and Urban Development (HUD) to extend mortgages to people who would not previously have qualified for them.

As you read, consider the following questions:

1. According to the author, what did the Federal Reserve Board do in the period 2001 to 2004 that dramatically increased the number of adjustable rate mortgages?

2. According to White, what were the four ways that the federal government encouraged the expansion of risky mortgages to unqualified borrowers?

3. In the author's view, why did Congress give Fannie Mae and Freddie Mac goals for low- and moderate-income borrowers?

Mortgage foreclosure rates in the United States have risen to the highest level since the Great Depression. The nation's two largest financial institutions, the government-sponsored mortgage purchasers and repackagers Fannie Mae [Federal National Mortgage Association] and Freddie Mac [Federal Home Loan Mortgage Corporation], have gone into bankruptcy-like "conservatorship." Several major investment banks, insurance companies, and commercial banks heavily tied to real estate lending have gone bankrupt outright or have been sold for cents on the dollar. Prices and trading volumes in mortgage-backed securities[1] have shrunk dramatically. Reluctance to lend has spread to other markets. To pre-

---

1. Mortgage-backed securities are debt obligations that represent claims to the cash flows from pools of mortgage loans, commonly on residential property.

pare the ground for a return to normalcy in American credit markets we must understand the character of the problems we currently face and how those problems arose.

What Did *Not* Happen

Some commentators (and both [2008] presidential candidates) have blamed the current financial mess on greed. But if an unusually high number of airplanes were to crash this year, would it make sense to blame gravity? No. Greed, like gravity, is a constant. It can't explain why the number of financial crashes is higher than usual. There has been no unusual epidemic of blackheartedness.

Others have blamed deregulation[2] or (in the words of one representative) "unregulated free-market lending run amok." Such an indictment is necessarily skimpy on the particulars, because there has actually been no recent dismantling of banking and financial regulations. Regulations were in fact intensified in the 1990s in ways that fed the development of the housing finance crisis, as discussed below. The last move in the direction of financial deregulation was the bipartisan Financial Services Modernization Act of 1999, also known as the Gramm-Leach-Bliley Act, signed by President [Bill] Clinton. That act opened the door for financial firms to diversify: a holding company that owns a commercial bank subsidiary may now also own insurance, mutual fund, and investment-bank subsidiaries. Far from contributing to the recent turmoil, the greater freedom allowed by the act has clearly been a blessing in containing it. Without it, JPMorgan Chase could not have acquired Bear Stearns, nor could Bank of America have acquired Merrill Lynch—acquisitions that avoided losses to Bear's and Merrill's bondholders. Without it, Goldman Sachs and Morgan Stanley could not have switched specialties to become bank holding companies when it became clear that they could no longer survive as investment banks.

2. Deregulation is the removal or easing of government rules and regulations in the economic system.

What *Did* Happen—and Why?

The actual causes of our financial troubles were unusual monetary policy moves and novel federal regulatory interventions. These poorly chosen public policies distorted interest rates and asset prices, diverted loanable funds into the wrong investments, and twisted normally robust financial institutions into unsustainable positions.

Let's review how the crisis has unfolded. Problems first surfaced in "exotic" or "flexible" home mortgage lending. Creative lenders and originators had expanded the volume of unconventional mortgages with high default risks (reflected in nonprime ratings),[3] which are the housing market's equivalent of junk bonds.[4] Unconventional mortgages helped to feed a run-up in condo and house prices. House prices peaked and turned downward. Borrowers with inadequate income relative to their debts, many of whom had either counted on being able to borrow against a higher house value in the future in order to help them meet their monthly mortgage payments, or on being able to "flip" the property at a price that would more than repay their mortgage, began to default. Default rates on nonprime mortgages rose to unexpected highs. The high risk on the mortgages came back to bite mortgage holders, the financial institutions to whom the monthly payments were owed. Firms directly holding mortgages saw reduced cash flows. Firms holding securitized mortgage bundles (often called "mortgage-backed securities") additionally saw the expectation of continuing reductions in cash flows reflected in declining market values for their securities. Uncertainty about future cash flows impaired the liquidity (resalability) of their securities.

Doubts about the value of mortgage-backed securities led naturally to doubts about the solvency of institutions heavily invested in those securities. Financial institutions that had

---

3. Nonprime mortgages are those given to individuals with a credit score, known as a FICO (Fair Isaac Corporation) score, under 620.
4. A junk bond is a bond rated BB or lower because it has a high risk of default.

stocked up on junk mortgages[5] and junk-mortgage-backed securities found their stock prices dropping. The worst cases, like Countrywide Financial, the investment banks Lehman Brothers and Merrill Lynch, and the government-sponsored mortgage purchasers Fannie Mae and Freddie Mac, went broke or had to find a last-minute purchaser to avoid bankruptcy. Firms heavily involved in guaranteeing mortgage-backed securities, like the insurance giant AIG, likewise ran aground. Suspect financial institutions began finding it difficult to borrow, because potential lenders could not confidently assess the chance that an institution might go bankrupt and be unable to pay them back. Credit flows among financial institutions became increasingly impeded by such solvency worries.

Given this sequence of events, the explanation of our credit troubles requires an explanation for the unusual growth of mortgage lending—particularly nonprime lending, which fed the housing bubble that burst—leading in turn to the unusual number of mortgage defaults, financial institution crashes, and attendant credit-market inhibitions.

There is no doubt that private miscalculation and imprudence have made matters worse for more than a few institutions. Such mistakes help to explain which particular firms have run into the most trouble. But to explain *industrywide* errors, we need to identify policy distortions capable of having industrywide effects.

We can group most of the unfortunate policies under two main headings: (1) Federal Reserve credit expansion that provided the means for unsustainable mortgage financing, and (2) mandates and subsidies to write riskier mortgages. The enumeration of regrettable policies below is by no means exhaustive.

5. Junk mortgages are those granted to people who have low credit scores and are at risk of defaulting on their mortgage.

41

Providing the Funds

In the recession of 2001, the Federal Reserve System, under Chairman Alan Greenspan, began aggressively expanding the U.S. money supply. Year-over-year growth in the M2[6] monetary aggregate rose briefly above 10 percent, and remained above 8 percent entering the second half of 2003. The expansion was accompanied by the Fed repeatedly lowering its target for the federal funds (interbank short-term) interest rate. The federal funds rate began 2001 at 6.25 percent and ended the year at 1.75 percent. It was reduced further in 2002 and 2003, in mid-2003 reaching a record low of 1 percent, where it stayed for a year. The *real* Fed funds rate was negative—meaning that nominal rates were lower than the contemporary rate of inflation—for two and a half years. In purchasing-power terms, during that period a borrower was not paying but rather gaining in proportion to what he borrowed. Economist Steve Hanke has summarized the result: "This set off the mother of all liquidity cycles and yet another massive demand bubble." . . .

The Fed's policy of lowering short-term interest rates not only fueled growth in the dollar volume of mortgage lending, but had unintended consequences for the *type* of mortgages written. By pushing very-short-term interest rates down so dramatically between 2001 and 2004, the Fed lowered short-term rates relative to 30-year rates. Adjustable-rate mortgages (ARMs), typically based on a one-year interest rate, became increasingly cheap relative to 30-year fixed-rate mortgages. Back in 2001, nonteaser ARM rates on average were 1.13 percent cheaper than 30-year fixed-mortgages (5.84 percent vs. 6.97 percent). By 2004, as a result of the ultra-low federal funds rate, the gap had grown to 1.94 percent (3.90 percent vs. 5.84 percent). Not surprisingly, increasing numbers of new

6. The M2 money supply consists of currency outside of the U.S. Treasury Federal Reserve Banks, and depository institution vaults; traveler's checks of nonbank issuers; demand deposits; and other checkable deposits; and time deposits at commercial banks, excluding large CDs (certificates of deposit).

mortgage borrowers were drawn away from mortgages with 30-year rates into ARMs. The share of new mortgages with adjustable rates, only one-fifth in 2001, had more than doubled by 2004. An adjustable-rate mortgage shifts the risk of refinancing at higher rates from the lender to the borrower. Many borrowers who took out ARMs implicitly (and imprudently) counted on the Fed to keep short-term rates low indefinitely. They have faced problems as their monthly payments have adjusted upward. The shift toward ARMs thus compounded the mortgage-quality problems arising from regulatory mandates and subsidies.

Researchers at the International Monetary Fund have corroborated the view that the Fed's easy-credit policy fueled the housing bubble. After estimating the sensitivity of U.S. housing prices and residential investment to interest rates, they find that "the increase in house prices and residential investment in the United States over the past six years would have been much more contained had short-term interest rates remained unchanged." Even Alan Greenspan, who otherwise protests his innocence, has acknowledged that "the 1 percent rate set in mid-2003 . . . lowered interest rates on adjustable-rate mortgages and may have contributed to the rise in U.S. home prices."

The excess investment in new housing has resulted in an overbuild of housing stock. Assuming that the federal government does not follow proposals (tongue-in-cheek or otherwise) that it should buy up and then raze excess houses and condos, or proposals to admit a large number of new immigrants, house prices and activity in the U.S. housing construction industry are going to remain depressed for a while. . . .

Mandates to Write Risky Mortgages

In 2001, the share of existing mortgages classified as nonprime (subprime or the intermediate category "Alt-A") was below 10 percent. That share began rising rapidly. The non-

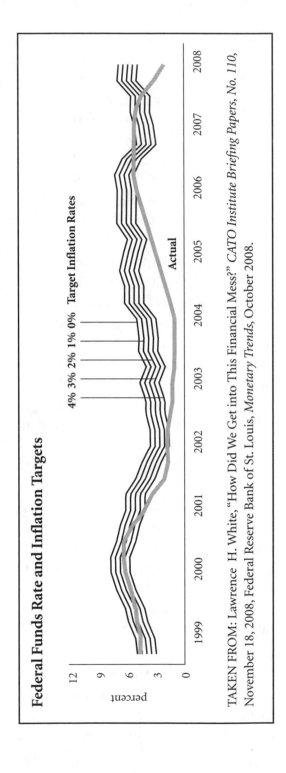

Federal Funds Rate and Inflation Targets

TAKEN FROM: Lawrence H. White, "How Did We Get into This Financial Mess?" *CATO Institute Briefing Papers, No. 110,* November 18, 2008, Federal Reserve Bank of St. Louis, *Monetary Trends,* October 2008.

prime share of all *new* mortgage originations rose close to 34 percent by 2006, bringing the nonprime share of existing mortgages to 23 percent. Meanwhile the quality of loans within the nonprime category declined, because a smaller share of nonprime borrowers made 20 percent down payments on their purchases.

The expansion in risky mortgages to under-qualified borrowers was an imprudence fostered by the federal government. As elaborated in the paragraphs to follow, there were several ways that Congress and the executive branch encouraged the expansion. The first way was loosening down-payment standards on mortgages guaranteed by the Federal Housing Administration [FHA]. The second was strengthening the Community Reinvestment Act [CRA]. The third was pressure on lenders by the Department of Housing and Urban Development. The fourth and most important way was subsidizing, through implicit taxpayer guarantees, the dramatic expansion of the government-sponsored mortgage buyers Fannie Mae and Freddie Mac; pointedly refusing to moderate the moral hazard problem of implicit guarantees or otherwise rein in the hyper-expansion of Fannie and Freddie; and increasingly pushing Fannie and Freddie to promote affordable housing through expanded purchases of nonprime loans to low-income applicants.

The Federal Housing Administration was founded in 1934 to insure mortgage loans made by private firms to qualifying borrowers. For a borrower to qualify, the FHA originally required—among other things—that the borrower provide a nonborrowed 20 percent down payment on the house being purchased. Private mortgage lenders like savings banks considered that to be a low down payment at the time. But private down payment requirements began falling toward the FHA level. The FHA reduced its requirements below 20 percent. Private mortgage insurance arose for non-FHA borrowers with down payments below 20 percent. Apparently concerned for bureaucratic reasons with preventing its "market share" from shrinking too far, the FHA began lowering its standards to stay below those of private lenders. By 2004 the required down payment on the FHA's most popular program had fallen to only 3 percent, and proposals were afoot in Congress to lower it to zero. Mortgages with very low down payments have had very high default rates.

The Community Reinvestment Act, first enacted in 1977, was relatively innocuous for its first 12 years or so, merely imposing reporting requirements on commercial banks regarding the extent to which they lent funds back into the neighborhoods where they gathered deposits. Congress amended the CRA in 1989 to make banks' CRA ratings public information. Further amendments in 1995 gave the CRA serious teeth: regulators could now deny a bank with a low CRA rating approval to merge with another bank—at a time when the arrival of interstate banking made such approvals especially valuable—or even to open new branches. Complaints from community organizations would now count against a bank's CRA rating. Groups like ACORN (the Association of Community Organizations for Reform Now) began actively pressuring banks to make loans under the threat that otherwise they would register complaints in order to deny the bank valuable approvals.

In response to the new CRA rules, some banks joined into partnerships with community groups to distribute millions in mortgage money to low-income borrowers previously considered noncreditworthy. Other banks took advantage of the newly authorized option to boost their CRA rating by purchasing special "CRA mortgage-backed securities," that is, packages of disproportionately nonprime loans certified as meeting CRA criteria and securitized by Freddie Mac. No doubt a small share of the total current crop of bad mortgages has come from CRA loans. But for the share of the increase in defaults that *has* come from the CRA-qualifying borrowers (who would otherwise have been turned down for lack of creditworthiness) rather than from, say, would-be condo-flippers on the outskirts of Las Vegas—the CRA bears responsibility. . . .

Meanwhile, beginning in 1993, officials in the Department of Housing and Urban Development began bringing legal actions against mortgage bankers that declined a higher percentage of minority applicants than white applicants. To avoid legal trouble, lenders began relaxing their down-payment and income qualifications.

Congress and HUD also pressured Fannie Mae and Freddie Mac. A 1992 law, as described by [Federal Reserve chairman Ben] Bernanke, "required the government-sponsored enterprises, Fannie Mae and Freddie Mac, to devote a large percentage of their activities to meeting affordable housing goals." Russell Roberts has cited some relevant numbers in the *Wall Street Journal*:

> Beginning in 1992, Congress pushed Fannie Mae and Freddie Mac to increase their purchases of mortgages going to low- and moderate-income borrowers. For 1996, the Department of Housing and Urban Development gave Fannie and Freddie an explicit target—42 percent of their mortgage financing had to go to borrowers with income below the median in their area. The target increased to 50 percent in 2000 and 52 percent in 2005.
>
> For 1996, HUD required that 12 percent of all mortgage purchases by Fannie and Freddie be "special affordable" loans, typically to borrowers with income less than 60% of their area's median income. That number was increased to 20% in 2000 and 22% in 2005. The 2008 goal was to be 28%. Between 2000 and 2005, Fannie and Freddie met those goals every year, funding hundreds of billions of dollars worth of loans, many of them subprime and adjustable-rate loans, and made to borrowers who bought houses with less than 10% down. . . .

The hyperexpansion of Fannie Mae and Freddie Mac was made possible by their implicit backing from the U.S. Treasury. To fund their enormous growth, Fannie Mae and Freddie Mac had to borrow huge sums in wholesale financial markets. Institutional investors were willing to lend to the government-sponsored mortgage companies cheaply—at rates only slightly above those on the Treasury's risk-free securities and well below those paid by other financial intermediaries—despite the risk of default that would normally attach to private firms holding such highly leveraged and poorly diversified portfolios. The investors were so willing only because they thought that the Treasury would repay them should Fannie or Freddie be unable. As it turns out, they were right. The Treasury did explicitly guarantee Fannie's and Freddie's debts when the two giants collapsed and were placed into conservatorship.

Congress was repeatedly warned by credible observers about the growing dangers posed by Fannie Mae's and Freddie Mac's implicit federal backing. . . .

Congress did nothing. Efforts to rein in Fannie and Freddie came to naught because the two giants had cultivated powerful friends on Capitol Hill. At hearings of the House Financial Services Committee in September 2003, regarding [George W.] Bush administration proposals to change the regulatory oversight of the GSEs,[7] in his opening statement Rep. Barney Frank (D-MA) defended the status quo arrangement on the grounds that it enabled Fannie and Freddie to lower mortgage interest rates for borrowers. . . .

Fix Bad Policies

The housing bubble and its aftermath arose from market distortions created by the Federal Reserve, government backing of Fannie Mae and Freddie Mac, the Department of Housing

---

7. GSEs are government-sponsored enterprises, a group of financial institutions created by the U.S. Congress.

and Urban Development, and the Federal Housing Authority. We are experiencing the unfortunate results of perverse government policies.

The traditional remedy for the severely mistaken investment policies of private firms—shut and dismantle those firms to stop the bleeding, free their assets and personnel to go where they can add value, and make room for firms with better entrepreneurial ideas—is as relevant as ever. A financial market in which failed enterprises like Freddie Mac or AIG are never shut down is like an *American Idol* contest in which the poorest singers never go home. The closure of Lehman Brothers (and the near-closure of Merrill Lynch), by raising the interest rate that the market charges to highly leveraged investment banks, forced Goldman Sachs and Morgan Stanley to change their business models drastically. The most effective and appropriate form of business regulation is regulation by profit and loss.

The long-term remedy for the severely mistaken government monetary and regulatory policies that have produced the current financial train wreck is similar. We need to identify and undo policies that distort housing and financial markets, and dismantle failed agencies whose missions require them to distort markets. We should be guided by recognizing the two chief errors that have been made. Cheap-money policies by the Federal Reserve System do not produce a sustainable prosperity. Hiding the cost of mortgage subsidies off-budget, as by imposing affordable housing regulatory mandates on banks and by providing implicit taxpayer guarantees on Fannie Mae and Freddie Mac bonds, does not give us more housing at nobody's expense.

"Lack of sensible supervision and regulation of . . . financial institutions . . . has been the core cause of this private sector created disaster, not excesses of regulation or of government policy."

The Banking Crisis Was Caused by a Lack of Regulation

Nouriel Roubini

Nouriel Roubini is professor of economics at the Stern School of Business, New York University, and chairman of RGE Monitor, an economic consulting firm. He was a senior economist for the Council of Economic Advisors and then a senior advisor to the U.S. Treasury Department during the Bill Clinton administration. In 2006, Roubini accurately predicted the coming financial crisis, a prediction that earned him the nickname "Dr. Doom" at the time. Because he was one of the few economists to see the coming disaster, he is considered a major figure in the debate about the economy.

In the following viewpoint, Roubini dismisses the claims of those who say the financial crisis was caused by government in-

Nouriel Roubini, "Who Is to Blame for the Mortgage Carnage and Coming Financial Disaster? Unregulated Free Market Fundamentalism Zealotry," *RGEMonitor*,March 19, 2007. Copyright © 2007 Roubini Global Economics, LLC. All rights reserved. Reproduced by permission.

terference and regulation of the free market. Rather, he argues, it was caused by a lack of regulation of the banking industry. Roubini lays the blame for this lack of regulation and the resulting economic catastrophe on the philosophy of laissez-faire nonintervention in free markets that was in place during the George W. Bush administration.

As you read, consider the following questions:

1. What does the author say the last three U.S. recessions had in common?

2. What are some of the practices Roubini attributes to lenders?

3. How does the author rebut the claim that Fannie Mae and Freddie Mac are responsible for the financial crisis?

Since a lot of nonsense and financially self-interested ideological spin will be written and said in the months and years to come it is important—from the beginning—to be clear about who is at fault for this utter housing and financial disaster. The answer is clear: the blame lies with free market zealots and fanatics and voodoo economics ideologues who captured US economic policy in the last six years [2001–2006] in the same way in which a bunch of neo-cons [new-style conservatives] high-jacked US foreign policy to bring "democracy" to the Middle East while instead leading the country into the Iraq and Mid-East quagmire and now disaster.

According to these ideologues—listen, for example, to [news host] Larry Kudlow extolling every evening on CNBC the virtue of unregulated wild-west cowboy capitalism—government is always utter evil and the economy could never have a financial or economic crisis if taxes are low, government spending is minimal and government intervention and regulation of the economy and of financial systems is inexistent. This nonsense about bubbles, financial crises and recessions being impossible unless the government over-regulates the economy and/or makes monetary policy mistakes is the main religious dogma of this cabal, an axis of ideological zealotry that goes from the WSJ [*Wall Street Journal*] editorial page to a gang of voodoo economic hacks and to some segments of financial television.

The truth is the contrary: unregulated free market capitalism that has no sensible rules, regulation and supervision and sensible countercyclical monetary and fiscal policies of financial markets leads to credit and asset bubbles, financial excesses and economic and financial crashes. . . .

Recessions Start as Regulation Stops

The reality of the last three US recessions—the 1990 recession, the 2001 recession and the coming 2007 hard landing—is that each of these recessions started when the government stopped regulating and supervising in moderate and sensible ways financial institutions and allowed credit and financial and investment bubbles to rise and fester until they ended up in bursting bubbles and leading to recessions.

Take the latest subprime[1] and mortgage disaster: the WSJ editorial page will certainly in due time blame the coming recession (that it now happens to predict as likely) on Congress meddling with markets, on predatory lending, on excessive regulation of what financial institutions do and on the moral hazard evils of expected bailouts of mortgage lenders and borrowers. But this argument is confusing totally cause and effect. The housing and mortgage and subprime bubble and bust did not occur because of government interference and regulation of free markets. It did instead occur because government regulators were asleep at the wheel while a bunch of voodoo

---

1. Subprime mortgages are those to individuals with poor credit histories (often below 600) who would not be able to qualify for conventional mortgages. Higher interest rates are charged on subprime mortgages than on conventional mortgages because of the increased risk of default for lenders.

priests of laissez-faire capitalism[2] were running US economic policy and let the housing and mortgage bubble fester. Blaming the now too late government crackdown on free market mortgage practices that were utterly reckless for the final bust and crash is like blaming the doctor for imposing bitter medicine to cure the disease of a reckless patient who lived in a bubble and spent the last few years on a diet of booze, drugs and artery clogging junk food. This latest mortgage carnage did not happen because of excessive over-regulation of markets by the government: it happened instead because—blinded by the anti-regulation dogmas of a bunch of priests of a voodoo religion—the government and regulators did nothing to sensibly regulate the housing and mortgage market and thus allowed this cancer to grow and fester. . . .

Lenders Engaged in Con Scheme

The last six years' housing and subprime mortgage bubble and bust had little to do with excessive government intervention. . . . Instead they had all to do with the lack of any basic sensible government regulation of the mortgage market, regulation in practice rather than in theory. Dozens of new subprime lenders emerged and were allowed to lend via monstrous credit practices—liar or NINJA loans,[3] no down-payment loans, interest rate only loans, negative amortization loans,[4] teaser rates, option ARMs[5] with no limits or con-

2. Laissez-faire capitalism is a political philosophy promoting limited or no government regulation in business matters.
3. A NINJA loan is a subprime loan issued to a buyer with no income, no job, and no assets.
4. A negative amortization loan is one where the payment by the borrower is less than the interest due and the difference is added to the loan balance. Thus, over time, the debt increases rather than is reduced, as in conventional mortgages.
5. An option ARM is an adjustable rate mortgage that typically offers four choices for repayment: a fully amortizing (eliminating by paying off over a period of time) 30-year payment, in which both principal and interest are paid on a 30-year schedule; a fully amortizing 15-year payment, in which both principal and interest are paid on a 15-year schedule; an interest-only payment, in which only the interest portion of the mortgage is paid, and not the principal; a minimum payment, a widely-picked option in which the payment is set for 12 months at a low introductory rate. After that, payment changes are made annually and a payment cap limits how much it can increase or decrease each year.

trols—that should have never been allowed in the first place. Even now that regulators are starting to crack down on the most patent monstrosities such as zero down-payment and no documentation of income, jobs and assets the voodoo priests and their acolytes in the mortgage industry are starting to blame the government for interfering with free market practices: in their ideological view there were optimal reasons for all of such practices: in market fundamentalism if such practices emerged there was a good reason for them and now the government interfering with these monstrosities will cause a credit crunch that will damage the mortgage market and cause a nasty credit crunch that will lead to an economy-wide recession. What a bunch of nonsense and self-interested baloney!

These practices instead emerged because the voodoo free market system of financial incentives for lenders—deceive borrowers with predatory practices, originate reckless mortgages to pile up fees, then securitize those mortgages and shove them on some other investors who had no clue of which toxic waste they were buying—became a whole con scheme. The way a senior and unnamed market participant put it, in a bit exaggerated terms, this was "an unregulated scam where a bunch of con artists fooled a bunch of clueless deadbeat borrowers".

So do not blame excessive government regulation; it was the lack of any basic regulation that created the bubble. Do not blame Congress for being the cause of the coming credit crunch because of its totally appropriate predatory lending investigations and soon legislation. If such legislation will lead—as some recent analyses have suggested—to the disappearance of one third of the subprime mortgage market, so be it, as part of these subprime loans were deceptive, predatory and should have never been made in the first place. Lenders were systematically deceiving poor and uninformed borrowers, many of which were minorities who had no clue of what they were getting into. Suppose you were a poor African American or Hispanic or a white poor with low income and no assets who wanted to pursue the American Dream of home ownership and you did not qualify for a regular mortgage because of your low income. No problem—told you the mortgage broker—we will give you a NINJA (no income, no job and assets) or liar loan, i.e. a loan with no documentation of your income and assets. You [could] not afford any down-payment because of little assets? No problem, as we will let you to put zero down-payment so that you start with zero equity in your home. You could not afford principal payments? No problem, as we will give you an interest-only loan. You could not afford a fixed rate mortgage? We will give you a 2-28 ARM [adjustable rate mortgage] where the rate is fixed at low level for two years and then you move to much higher market rates. You [could not] afford even that? We will give you a teaser rate for a little while. You could not afford even that? We will let you capitalize interest on a higher face value of the mortgage for a while so that you will have negative amortization and you pile up negative equity on your home from the very beginning. And the poor, hapless and clueless borrowers said yes to all of this as the lender never told him that after two years its debt servicing rate would balloon by 500% once he/she had to start paying high market rates and principal on an ever increasing—not decreasing—stock of mortgage debt. So do not blame Congress for necessary legislation on predatory lending for causing the current credit crunch; it was the lack of such legislation in the first place that allowed millions of mortgages that should have not been originated in the first place to mushroom without control.

Also, did the originators care or have any interest or incentive to warn the borrower that he/she could not afford such predatory and deceptive mortgages? No way, as the originator would get very fat originations fees/commissions, then package this toxic waste into mortgage backed securities,[6] get

6. A security is an investment instrument issued by a corporation, government, or other organization (excluding insurance policies and fixed annuities) that represents financial value. Securities can be debt (such as banknotes or bonds), equity (such as stocks), or derivatives (such as futures, options, or swaps).

Bank Targets Blacks

As she describes it, Beth Jacobson and her fellow loan officers at Wells Fargo Bank "rode the stagecoach from hell" for a decade, systematically singling out blacks in Baltimore and suburban Maryland for high-interest subprime mortgages.

These loans, Baltimore officials have claimed in a federal lawsuit against Wells Fargo, tipped hundreds of homeowners into foreclosure and cost the city tens of millions of dollars in taxes and city services.

Wells Fargo, Ms. Jacobson said in an interview, saw the black community as fertile ground for subprime mortgages, as working-class blacks were hungry to be a part of the nation's home-owning mania. Loan officers, she said, pushed customers who could have qualified for prime loans into subprime mortgages.

Michael Powell,
New York Times, *June 7, 2007.*

a nice rating on that garbage from oligopolistic [system where a few large firms dominate the market] credit rating agencies whose income derived from giving a high rating to this junk—under the pretense that tens of thousands of piles of toxic waste would turn by miracle into gourmet food—and then sell this securitized toxic junk as if it was fresh roses to even more clueless "savvy" investors desperately searching for yield and being dumbly ignorant of the risks that they were taking. These investors were not innocent victims; they were blinded by their own search-for-yield greed and did not bother to figure out non-transparent and totally opaque new financial instruments may be toxic waste. . . .

Fannie and Freddie Not to Blame

Also, please do not blame the GSEs [government sponsored enterprises] (Fannie [the Federal National Mortgage Association] and Freddie [the Federal Home Loan Mortgage Corporation]) for this mess even if the GSEs do have very different problems that need to be addressed. The GSEs were bashed for years by [Federal Reserve chairman Alan] Greenspan, Treasury, [Federal Reserve chairman Ben] Bernanke and a wide variety of observers for their excessive size and role in the mortgage market (securitization[7] and guarantees of mortgages), for how they were managing their risks and for the potential moral hazard deriving from an alleged implicit bailout guarantee that allowed them to borrow at quasi-sovereign rates. Indeed some of these critiques of the GSEs do have some merit.

But the paradoxical effect of the backlash against the GSEs has been that in the last few years these institutions have significantly reduced their role in securitizing and guaranteeing mortgages. Specifically Fannie and Freddie significantly reduced their presence in the MBS [mortgage-backed securities][8] market, especially among subprime mortgages and the MBS related to them. Reacting to the persistent arguments from many fronts that the two GSEs should reduce their role in the MBS market, in the last few years the job of originating and securitizing subprime mortgages and many near-prime mortgages was mostly taken over by private sector institutions. As the GSEs got out of this business, subprime lenders and other major financial institutions originated sub-prime and near-prime mortgages, repackaged them and securitized

7. Securitization is the process of aggregating similar types of investments, typically loans or mortgages, into a common pool, then selling that pool of investments.
8. A mortgage-backed security is a debt obligation to the cash flows from a pool of mortgage loans, commonly on residential property. These securities are created when a financial institution buys mortgages from a primary lender, sells them in a bundle to investors, and uses the monthly mortgage payments to pay the investors.

them into MBS then sold to investors and to CDOs.[9] So, the growth of subprime and near-prime toxic waste had little or nothing to do with the role of the GSE in the mortgage market. Fannie and Freddie may have many faults but this subprime disaster is certainly not one of them. So beware of misleading attempts to blame the GSEs and moral hazard distortions from their perceived semi-public status in contributing to this subprime and mortgage disaster. . . .

In a world where the leading ideology was to reduce regulation to a minimum, not only closing one's eyes on monster lending practices but rather actively praising them as brilliant financial innovations, bashing GSEs in the name of letting the superior private sector take a bigger role in monster housing finance, it is not a surprise that the biggest bubble in U.S. history was created, incentivated and allowed to fester until it imploded. Free market fundamentalist zealotry that did not understand that market capitalism needs some basic and sensible rules, regulation and supervision to control excesses, bubbles, greed and investors' manias and panics. . . .

Lack of Regulation Is to Blame

In summary, lack of sensible supervision and regulation of banks, mortgage lenders and other financial institutions—partly induced by an ideology of free market fundamentalism—has been the core cause of this private sector created disaster, not excesses of regulation or of government policy. Thus, to minimize the fiscal costs of cleaning up this mess, use of public funds should be carefully managed and targeted to help the true victims of this mess—borrowers duped by predatory lending practices—while avoiding any bail-out of the culprits of this mess. Privatizing profits in good times

9. Collateralized debt obligations (CDOs) are a type of security backed by a pool of bonds, loans, and other assets. CDOs are assigned different risk classes, or tranches, with senior tranches considered the safest securities. Interest and principal payments are made in order of seniority, so that junior tranches offer higher interest rates and lower prices to compensate for the additional risk of default.

while socializing losses in bad times is another form of reckless corporate welfare that generates moral hazard while fostering new bubbles. Ideological supply side voodoo zealots should not be allowed to spin a tale where evil government intervention caused this disaster. And the private sector institutions and investors that indulged in this unregulated reckless behavior should take their losses. Market economies are the best economic system but they work properly when private greed, manias, panics, stupidity and recklessness is tempered by sensible supervision and regulation. And may the unfolding mortgage disaster bury once and for all the neo-con supply side voodoo economics religion of unregulated free markets fundamentalism.

"Financial services were not deregulated during the Bush administration. If there ever was an 'era of deregulation' in the financial world, it ended long ago."

Deregulation Did Not Cause the Banking Crisis

James L. Gattuso

James L. Gattuso covers regulatory and telecommunications issues as senior research fellow at the Thomas A. Roe Institute for Economic Policy Studies at The Heritage Foundation, a conservative think tank.

According to Gattuso in the following viewpoint, contrary to attempts by some politicians to place blame on the George W. Bush administration for the financial crisis, there was no deregulation of financial services under this administration. The easing of banking restrictions took place at an earlier time, during the 1970s and 1980s. Gattuso contends that—rather than being a cause of the financial crisis—this earlier deregulation has actually helped mitigate some of the effects of the crisis.

As you read, consider the following questions:

1. When does the author believe an era of deregulation existed?

2. What act does Bill Clinton argue did not contribute to the crisis, according to Gattuso?

3. What evidence does the author cite to support his argument that the Clinton administration was more deregulatory than the Bush administration?

Easy answers are seldom correct ones. That principle seems to be at work as the nation struggles to discover the causes of the financial crisis now rocking the economy. Looking for a simple and politically convenient villain, many politicians have blamed deregulation[1] by the [George W.] Bush Administration.

House Speaker Nancy Pelosi, for instance, stated [in September 2008] that "the Bush Administration's eight long years of failed deregulation policies have resulted in our nation's largest bailout ever, leaving the American taxpayers on the hook potentially for billions of dollars." Similarly, presidential candidate Barack Obama asserted in the second presidential debate that "the biggest problem in this whole process was the deregulation of the financial system."

But there is one problem with this answer: Financial services were not deregulated during the Bush Administration. If there ever was an "era of deregulation" in the financial world, it ended long ago. And the changes made then are for the most part non-controversial today.

Regulatory Structures Never in Doubt

In a literal sense, financial services were never "deregulated," nor was there ever a serious attempt to do so. Few analysts have ever proposed the elimination of the regulatory struc-

1. Deregulation is the removal or easing of government rules and regulations in the economic system.

tures in place to ensure the soundness and transparency of banks. Simply put, the job of bank examiner was never threatened.

More typically, of course, the word *deregulation* has been used as shorthand to describe the repeal or easing of particular rules. To the extent there was a heyday of such deregulation, it was in the 1970s and 1980s. It was at this time that economists—and consumer activists—began to question many long-standing restrictions on financial services.

The most important such restrictions were rules banning banks from operating in more than one state. Such rules were largely eliminated by 1994 through state and federal action. Few observers lament their passing today, and because regional and nationwide banks are far better able to balance risk, this "deregulation" has helped mitigate, rather than contribute to, the instability of the system.

Gramm-Leach-Bliley and Beyond

The next major "deregulation" of financial services was the repeal of the Depression-era prohibition on banks engaging in the securities business. The ban was formally ended by the 1999 Gramm-Leach-Bliley Act, which followed a series of decisions by regulators easing its impact.

While not without controversy, the net effect of Gramm-Leach-Bliley has likely been to alleviate rather than further the current financial crisis.

In fact, President Bill Clinton—who signed the reform bill into law—defended the legislation in a recent interview, saying, "I don't see that signing that bill had anything to do with the current crisis. Indeed, one of the things that has helped stabilize the current situation as much as it has is the purchase of Merrill Lynch by Bank of America, which was much smoother than it would have been if I hadn't signed that bill."

In 2000, Congress also passed legislation that, among other things, clarified that certain kinds of financial instruments were not regulated by the Commodity Futures Trading Commission (CFTC). Among these were "credit default swaps,"[2] which have played a role in [2008]'s meltdown. Whether this law constituted "deregulation" is not clear, since the pre-legislation status of these instruments was uncertain. Nor is it a given that CFTC regulation of their trading would have avoided the financial crisis. In fact, many policymakers, including Clinton Treasury Secretary Robert Rubin, argued that their regulation would do more harm than good.

In the nine years since that legislation—including the eight years of the Bush presidency—Congress has enacted no further legislation easing burdens [on the] financial services industry.

Regulatory Agency Trends

But what of the regulatory agencies? Did they pursue a deregulatory agenda during the Bush Administration? Again, the answer seems to be no.

In terms of rulemaking—the promulgation of specific rules by regulatory agencies—the Securities and Exchange Commission (SEC) is by far the most active among agencies in the financial realm. Based on data from the Government Accountability Office, the SEC completed 23 proceedings since the beginning of the Bush Administration that resulted in a substantive and major change (defined as an economic effect of $100 million or more) in regulatory burdens. Of those, only eight—about a third—lessened burdens. Perhaps surprisingly, the Bush record in this regard is actually less deregulatory than that of the Clinton Administration, which during its second term lessened burdens in nine out of 20 such rulemaking proceedings.

2. A credit default swap (CDS) is a transaction where the buyer of a bond or loan makes payments to the seller, who guarantees the creditworthiness of the product. The buyer receives a payment from the seller if the product goes into default.

No Era of Deregulation

Many journalists claim that the U.S. economy since the late 1970s has been very free, with little regulation; that this absence of regulation has caused markets to fail; that there was a consensus in favor of little regulation; and that now this consensus is fading. On all these counts, the reports are false. Specifically, the U.S. economy has not been free since before the New Deal of the 1930s. Even before the 1930s, the U.S. economy was "mixed"— that is, a combination of economic freedom and government regulation—and Franklin Roosevelt's New Deal altered the mix substantially toward regulation and away from freedom. The deregulation of the late 1970s and 1980s reversed some of the regulations that came with the New Deal and some that preceded it, but the net amount of regulation has been much higher in the alleged era of deregulation than it was during the post-National Recovery Administration New Deal.

David R. Henderson,
Cato Policy Report, *November/December 2008.*

Other financial agencies have been far less active in making formal rule changes. The Federal Reserve reports five major rulemakings in the database since 1996—four of which were deregulatory. The only rule change reported by the Federal Deposit Insurance Corporation and the Controller of the Currency is the 1997 adoption of new capital reserve standards, an action with mixed consequences.

Of course, much of the work of regulators takes place in day-to-day activities rather than in formal rulemaking activities. For that reason, it is also helpful to look at the budgets of regulators.

These also show little sign of reduced regulatory activity during the Bush years. The total budget of federal finance and banking regulators (excluding the SEC) increased from approximately $2 billion in FY [fiscal year] 2000 to almost $2.3 billion in FY 2008 in constant 2000 dollars. The SEC's budget during the same time period jumped from $357 million in 2000 to a whopping $629 million in 2008. During the same time period, total staffing at these agencies remained steady, at close to 16,000.

A False Narrative

In the wake of the financial crisis gripping the nation, it is tempting to blame "deregulation" for triggering the problem. After all, if the meltdown were caused by the ill-advised elimination of necessary rules, the answer would be easy: Restore those rules.

But that storyline is simply not true. Not only was there was little deregulation of financial services during the Bush years, but most of the regulatory reforms achieved in earlier years mitigated, rather than contributed to, the crisis.

This, of course, does not mean that no regulatory changes should be considered. In the wake of the current crisis, debate over the scope and method of regulation in financial markets is inevitable and, in fact, necessary. But this cannot be a debate over returning to a regulatory Nirvana that never existed. Any new regulatory system would be just that—complete with all the uncertainty and prospects for unintended consequences that define such a system. Policymakers must not pretend otherwise.

> "Compensation practices had gotten totally out of hand and spurred financial people to aim for a lot of short-term money without worrying about the eventual consequences."

Excessive Compensation Packages Contributed to the Banking Crisis

Paul Volcker

Paul Volcker, an economist, was U.S. Federal Reserve Board chairman from 1979 to 1987. He is currently chairman of President Barack Obama's Economic Recovery Advisory Board.

In the following viewpoint Volcker states that the banking crisis is not an ordinary crisis—rather, it is one that threatens the stability of the entire global financial system. He explains that the crisis originated when Asian economies had surplus funds to invest, and U.S. financiers needed to develop additional investment opportunities to take advantage of these funds. Because residential housing was the largest opportunity, financiers developed a way of creating class A mortgages by combining risky mortgages with prime mortgages and calling the whole package a class A mortgage. Volcker contends that this occurred

Paul Volcker, "Not an Ordinary Recession," *The Big Picture*, February 22, 2009.

and was allowed to continue because people were making a lot of money doing this, and, because of the complexity of the deals, few people understood the risks.

As you read, consider the following questions:

1. What are some of the imbalances in the world economy the author cites that created the environment that led to risky mortgages?

2. What is the primary characteristic of the financial system of thirty years ago that Volcker says should be returned to?

3. What is the distinction that the author makes between potential compensation in the traditional commercial banking system vs. the capital market system?

This is not an ordinary recession. I have never, in my lifetime, seen a financial problem of this sort. It has the makings of something much more serious than an ordinary recession where you go down for a while and then you bounce up and it's partly a monetary—but a self-correcting—phenomenon. The ordinary recession does not bring into question the stability and the solidity of the whole financial system. Why is it that this is so much more profound a crisis? I'm not saying it's going to get anywhere as serious as the Great Depression, but that was not an ordinary business cycle either.

Incentives Led to Risk

This phenomenon can be traced back at least five or six years. We had, at that time, a major underlying imbalance in the world economy. The American proclivity to consume was in full force. Our consumption rate was about 5% higher, relative to our GNP [gross national product] or what our production normally is. Our spending—consumption, investment, government—was running about 5% or more above our production, even though we were more or less at full employment.

You had the opposite in China and Asia, generally, where the Chinese were consuming maybe 40% of their GNP—we consumed 70% of our GNP. They had a lot of surplus dollars because they had a lot of exports. Their exports were feeding our consumption and they were financing it very nicely with very cheap money. That was a very convenient but unsustainable situation. The money was so easy, funds were so easily available that there was, in effect, a kind of incentive to finding ways to spend it.

When we finished with the ordinary ways of spending it—with the help of our new profession of financial engineering—we developed ways of making weaker and weaker mortgages. The biggest investment in the economy was residential housing. And we developed a technique of manufacturing class D mortgages but putting them in packages which the financial engineers said were class A.

So there was an enormous incentive to take advantage of this bit of arbitrage[1]—cheap money, poor mortgages but saleable mortgages. A lot of people made money through this process. I won't go over all the details, but you had then a normal business cycle on top of it. It was a period of enthusiasm. Everybody was feeling exuberant. They wanted to invest and spend.

You had a bubble first in the stock market and then in the housing market. You had a big increase in housing prices in the United States, held up by these new mortgages. It was true in other countries as well, but particularly in the United States. It was all fine for a while, but of course, eventually, the house

1. Arbitrage is a strategy in which investors profit from temporary discrepancies between the prices of the stocks comprising an index (stocks grouped together so their performance can be measured) and the price of a futures contract on that index. By buying either the stocks or the futures contract and selling the other, an investor can sometimes exploit market inefficiency for a profit.

prices leveled off and began going down. At some point people began getting nervous and the whole process stopped because they realized these mortgages were no good.

You might ask how it went on as long as it did. The grading agencies didn't do their job and the banks didn't do their job and the accountants went haywire. I have my own take on this. There were two things that were particularly contributory and very simple. Compensation practices had gotten totally out of hand and spurred financial people to aim for a lot of short-term money without worrying about the eventual consequences. And then there was this obscure financial engineering that none of them understood, but all their mathematical experts were telling them to trust. These two things carried us over the brink.

One of the saddest days of my life was when my grandson—and he's a particularly brilliant grandson—went to college. He was good at mathematics. And after he had been at college for a year or two I asked him what he wanted to do when he grew up. He said, "I want to be a financial engineer." My heart sank. Why was he going to waste his life on this profession?

A year or so ago, my daughter had seen something in the paper, some disparaging remarks I had made about financial engineering. She sent it to my grandson, who normally didn't communicate with me very much. He sent me an email, "Grandpa, don't blame it on us! We were just following the orders we were getting from our bosses." The only thing I could do was send him back an email, "I will not accept the Nuremberg excuse" [used by Nazi war criminals at the Nuremberg trials that they were just following orders].

There was so much opaqueness, so many complications and misunderstandings involved in very complex financial engineering by people who, in my opinion, did not know financial markets. They knew mathematics. They thought financial markets obeyed mathematical laws. They have found out differently now. You know, they all said these events only happen once every hundred years. But we have "once every hundred years" events happening every year or two, which tells me something is the matter with the analysis.

The System Is Broken

So I think we have a problem which is not an ordinary business cycle problem. It is much more difficult to get out of and it has shaken the foundations of our financial institutions. The system is broken. I'm not going to linger over what to do about it. It is very difficult. It is going to take a lot of money and a lot of losses in the banking system. It is not unique to the United States. It is probably worse in the UK and it is just about as bad in Europe and it has infected other economies as well. Canada is relatively less infected, for reasons that are consistent with the direction in which I think the financial markets and financial institutions should go.

So I'll jump over the short-term process, which is how we get out of the mess, and consider what we should be aiming for when we get out of the mess. That, in turn, might help instruct the kind of action we should be taking in the interim to get out of it.

In the United States, in the UK, as well—and potentially elsewhere—things are partly being held together by totally extraordinary actions by a central bank. In the United States, it's the Federal Reserve, in London, the Bank of England. They are providing direct credit to markets in massive volume, in a way that contradicts all the traditions and laws that have governed central banking behavior for a hundred years.

So what are we aiming for? I mention this because I recently chaired a report on this. It was part of the so-called Group of 30,[2] which has got some attention. It's a long and rather turgid report but let me simplify what the conclusion is, which I will state more boldly than the report itself does.

2. The Group of Thirty, established in 1978, is a private, nonprofit, international body composed of very senior representatives of the private and public sectors and academia.

"'WallStreet' street sign with cross walk light reading 'Get Real'" cartoon by Carole Cable

Two Different Institutions Needed

In the future, we are going to need a financial system which is not going to be so prone to crisis and certainly will not be prone to the severity of a crisis of this sort. Financial systems always fluctuate and go up and down and have crises, but let's not have a big crisis that undermines the whole economy. And if that's the kind of financial system we want and should have, it's going to be different from the financial system that has developed in the last 20 years.

What do I mean by different? I think a primary characteristic of the system ought to be a strong, traditional, commercial banking–type system. Probably we ought to have some very large institutions—or at least that's the way the market is going—whose primary purpose is a kind of fiduciary responsibility to service consumers, individuals, businesses and governments by providing outlets for their money and by providing credit. They ought to be the core of the credit and financial system.

This kind of system was in place in the United States thirty years ago and is still in place in Canada, and may have provided support for the Canadian system during this particularly difficult time. I'm not arguing that you need an oligopoly [a small group of sellers that dominate a market] to the extent you have one in Canada, but you do know by experience that these big commercial banking institutions will be protected by the government, de facto. No government has been willing to permit these institutions, or the creditors and depositors to these institutions, to be damaged. They recognize that the damage to the economy would be too great.

What has happened recently just underscores that. And I think we're at the point where we can no longer fool ourselves by saying that is not the case. The government will support these institutions, which in turn implies a closer supervision and regulation of those institutions, a more effective regulation than we've had, at least in the United States, in the recent past. And that may involve a lot of different agencies and so forth. I won't get into that.

But I think it does say that those institutions should not engage in highly risky entrepreneurial activity. That's not their job because it brings into question the stability of the institution. They may make a lot of money and they may have a lot of fun, in the short run. It may encourage pursuit of a profit in the short run. But it is not consistent with the stability that those institutions should be about. It's not consistent at all with avoiding conflict of interest.

These institutions that have arisen in the United States and the UK that combine hedge funds,[3] equity funds,[4] large proprietary trading with commercial banks, have enormous conflicts of interest. And I think the conflicts of interest contribute to their instability. So I would say let's get rid of that. Let's have big and small commercial banks and protect them— it's the service part of the financial system.

And then we have the other part, which I'll call the capital market system, which by and large isn't directly dealing with customers. They're dealing with each other. They're trading. They're about hedge funds and equity funds. And they have a function in providing fluid markets and innovating and providing some flexibility, and I don't think they need to be so highly regulated. They're not at the core of the system, unless they get really big. If they get really big then you have to regulate them, too. But I don't think we need to have close regulation of every peewee hedge fund in the world.

So you have this bifurcated—in a sense—financial system that implies a lot about regulation and national governments. If you're going to have an open system, you have got to get much more cooperation and coordination from different countries. I think that's possible, given what we're going through. You've got to do something about the infrastructure of the system and you have to worry about the credit rating agencies.

These banks were relying on credit rating agencies while putting these big packages of securities[5] together and selling them. They had practically—they would never admit this—

3. A hedge fund is a pooled private investment fund that seeks to maximize returns with strategies that include unconventional investments and investments that cannot quickly be converted to cash, such as real estate.
4. An equity fund is a mutual fund that invests primarily in stocks, usually common stocks.
5. A security is an investment instrument issued by a corporation, government, or other organization (excluding insurance policies and fixed annuities) that represents financial value. Securities can be debt (such as banknotes or bonds), equity (such as stocks), or derivatives (such as futures, options, or swaps).

given up credit departments in their own institutions that were sophisticated and well-developed. That was a cost centre—why do we need it, they thought. Obviously that hasn't worked out very well.

We have to look at the accounting system. We have to look at the system for dealing with derivatives[6] and how they're settled. So there are a lot of systemic issues. The main point I'm making is that we want to emerge from this with a more stable system. It will be less exciting for many people, but it will not warrant—I don't think the present system does, either—$50 million dollar paydays in that central part of the system. Or even $25 or $100 million dollar paydays. If somebody can go out and gamble and make that money, okay. But don't gamble with the public's money. And that's an important distinction.

It's interesting that what I'm arguing for looks more like the Canadian system than the American system. When we delivered this report in a press conference, people said, "Oh you mean, banks won't be able to have hedge funds? What are you talking about?" That same day, Citigroup announced, "We want to get rid of all that stuff. We now realize it was a mistake. We want to go back to our roots and be a real commercial bank." I don't know whether they'll do that or not. But the fact that one of the leading proponents of the other system basically said, "We give up. It's not the right system," is interesting.

---

6. A derivative is a financial instrument whose value is derived from an underlying asset, index, event, value, or condition. The derivative itself is merely a contract to exchange cash or assets over time based on fluctuations in the underlying assets. Most derivatives are characterized by high leverage, or debt.

> *"[JPMorgan Chase & Co.] have long adhered to compensation practices that were designed to reward long-term performance, not just revenues, and aimed to align employee and shareholder interests."*

Not All Banks Have Excessive Executive Compensation Packages

Jamie Dimon

Jamie Dimon is chairman and chief executive officer of JPMorgan Chase & Co. as well as a director of the New York Federal Reserve. He was named one of the world's one hundred most influential people by Time *magazine in 2006 and 2009.*

Although admitting that American citizens are justifiably concerned about the compensation practices across the financial services industry, in the following viewpoint Dimon contends that the compensation system for all employees at JPMorgan Chase was entirely appropriate in 2008. To support this, he reports that compensation declined in 2008 by more than 60 percent for the most senior group of executives.

Jamie Dimon, "Testimony of Jamie Dimon, Chairman & CEO, JPMorgan Chase & Co., House Financial Services Committee," February 11, 2009. Reproduced by permission of the author.

As you read, consider the following questions:

1. What were some of the features of JPMorgan Chase's compensation program, even prior to 2008, according to Dimon?

2. The author states that compensation across JPMorgan Chase was sharply reduced in 2008. What are some of the declines in employee compensation that he cites?

3. What solution does Dimon offer to solve problems in the current financial regulatory system, which he describes as fragmented and overly complex?

I know that many Americans are concerned about compensation practices across the financial services industry—and I think some of those concerns are quite legitimate. At JPMorgan Chase, we have long adhered to compensation practices that were designed to reward long-term performance, not just revenues, and aimed to align employee and shareholder interests. Before the TARP [Troubled Asset Relief Program, also known as the stimulus package] program was conceived, we used a multi-year approach to compensation, weighed risk management as part of our performance evaluations, had a bonus recoupment policy beyond that required under Sarbanes-Oxley,[1] and did not use golden parachutes[2] or many other perquisites. We have always paid a significant percentage of our incentive compensation in stock (50 percent for our most senior management group) and require this group to hold 75 percent of their stock until retirement.

And for us, incentive compensation is not a perquisite given exclusively to senior officers and investment bankers. It is part of our regular compensation given to employees across

---

1. The Sarbanes-Oxley Act was enacted following a number of corporate and accounting scandals and set more rigorous accounting standards for publicly traded companies.

2. A golden parachute is a clause in an employment agreement guaranteeing an executive lucrative severance benefits.

the firm, including retail branch and credit card personnel, technology experts, and compliance and support professionals. Each employee is paid based on a combination of individual performance, business unit performance and the performance of the firm as a whole.

I took no bonus for 2008 in any form, cash, stock, or options.[3] I judged that it was appropriate for me, as the leader of a major financial firm in the current environment, to forgo a bonus last year. Many of our employees took significant cuts in compensation, and the more senior executives took the larger percentage cuts. For our most senior management group, incentive compensation declined more than 60 percent. For the firm as a whole, average incentive compensation per employee was down 38 percent. (Average *cash* incentive compensation was down by 43 percent.) This is true even though, during one of the most tumultuous periods our economy has ever experienced, we earned a profit in every quarter and executed the Bear Stearns and Washington Mutual transactions.[4] Our employees worked harder than ever and performed admirably for the company and for clients under enormously challenging conditions in 2008. I believe the compensation we paid them was appropriate.

State of the Industry

Before I conclude, I should address the [U.S. House Financial Services] Committee's request for comment on the state of the financial industry. These are obviously challenging times. The government, in my view, has taken bold and necessary steps to keep this crisis from becoming something that none of us would want to imagine. Congress will be tackling many more challenges in the months ahead and we stand ready to work with you on the range of issues confronting the financial ser-

3. Employee stock options are the opportunity to purchase stock, or have stock awarded, under favorable terms.
4. These two entities were bought by JPMorgan Chase.

JPMorgan Chase Cuts Bonuses

JPMorgan Chase is to raise salaries and cut bonuses for more than 12,000 bankers around the world in a sign that financial groups are scrambling to defuse public anger at excessive pay while trying to avoid an exodus of talent. . . .

The salary increases will be accompanied by corresponding cuts in bonuses to leave bankers' compensation, and JPMorgan's wage bill, unchanged, said people close to the matter.

Francesco Guerrera and Julie MacIntosh,
Financial Times, *July 25, 2009.*

vices sector and our economy as a whole. One issue I do want to touch on briefly is the need for regulatory modernization. For in my view, long-term recovery will elude the financial industry unless we modernize our financial regulatory system and address the regulatory weaknesses that recent events have uncovered.

The ongoing financial crisis has exposed significant deficiencies in our current regulatory system, which is fragmented and overly-complex. Maintaining separate regulatory agencies across banking, securities[5] and insurance businesses is not only inefficient, but also denies any one agency access to complete information needed to regulate large diversified institutions effectively and maintain stability across the financial system. It also results in uneven and inequitable regulation of similar activities and products across different institutions.

5. Securities are investment instruments issued by a government or corporation representing financial value in that entity.

I am in complete agreement with Chairman [Barney] Frank that Congress and the President should move ahead quickly to establish a systemic risk regulator. In the short-term, this would allow us to begin to address some of the underlying weaknesses in our system and fill the gaps in regulation that contributed to the current situation.

As part of a longer-term modernization discussion, we stand ready to work with Congress and others to think through any number of complex issues. But waiting for the larger debate over regulatory reform to play out could take months. Every credible regulatory modernization plan includes the creation of a systemic risk regulator, and everyone agrees that this needs to be done—and done right away. I hope Congress will act to get this critical building block in place.

> "What really caused the magnitude of
> the current financial crisis . . . was the
> amount of leverage used in the housing
> market and mortgage backed securities
> derived from it."

The Banking Crisis Was Caused by Excessive Debt

Andy Singh

*Andy Singh writes articles on the financial industry and invest-
ing for Seeking Alpha, an investing Web site. He also writes
Savingtoinvest.com, a Web log.*

*In the following viewpoint, Singh explains how the amount
of debt that home buyers were taking on was the root cause of
the financial crisis. Many homes were purchased with little down
payment, and the housing boom caused prices to almost double
in some markets before the collapse. These mortgages were passed
along in bundles to investors, and when housing prices fell, homeowners owed more than their property was worth, financial
institutions were left with loans that would not be repaid, and
investors had an investment that had decreased in value. Singh*

Andy Singh, "Leverage 101: The Real Cause of the Financial Crisis," *Seeking Alpha*, September 25, 2008. Reproduced by permission of the author.

concludes that debt, or leverage, is not a bad thing—it was the excessive level of debt, at a thirty-to-one ratio, that created the problem.

As you read, consider the following questions:

1. As described by the author, what are potential rates of return for a home purchase with no leverage, partial leverage, and maximum leverage?

2. What happens in these three scenarios, according to Singh, if the value of the house declines by thirty thousand dollars, instead of appreciating in value?

3. What happens when an investment bank puts down $1 million for $30 million worth of mortgages and housing prices fall, according to the author?

Much of the current financial market crisis is blamed on two main factors—poor risk management by company executives and the ultra-depressed housing market. Company management is paying the penalty with the most failed CEOs [chief executive officers] fired and years of lawsuits and regulatory probes ahead for implicated senior executives. The second factor, a depressed housing market, in itself is not new. Housing is cyclical and every 10 years or so we have a downturn followed by a boom. Despite this being a much more severe downturn, you also have to remember prices almost doubled (boomed) before the collapse.

Excessive Leverage

What really caused the magnitude of the current financial crisis, in my opinion, was the amount of *leverage*[1] *used in the housing market and mortgage backed securities*[2] *derived from it.*

1. Leverage is the use of debt to grow an investment.
2. A mortgage-backed security is created when a financial institution buys mortgages from a primary lender, sells these in a bundle to investors, and uses the monthly mortgage payments to pay the investors.

Leverage is a double-edged sword that is a powerful ally during boom times, but can quickly become your worst enemy during the ensuing bust. The collapse or bailout of some of our most highly regarded financial institutions—Fannie Mae (FNM) [the Federal National Mortgage Association], AIG (AIG), Lehman Brothers and Merrill Lynch (MER)—was squarely due to leverage.

What is leverage and how does it work? Below is a simplified example using three scenarios:

1. *No leverage.* Assume I purchase outright (in cash) a home valued at $100,000. If that house increases in value by $10,000 in one year, my *rate of return* (appreciation) against my $100,000 cash outlay (down payment) is 10% ($10,000/$100,000). Not bad.

2. *Partial Leverage.* Now assume that I purchase a home valued at $100,000 and only contribute $10,000 as a down payment and finance the remaining $90,000 at 6% (equivalent to $5,400 in annual interest). If the house increases in value by $10,000 in one year, my *rate of return* (appreciation) on my outlay (down payment plus the interest costs) is $10,000 / ($10,000 + $5,400) = 65%. So, through leverage of about 10 to 1, I was able to increase my rate of return significantly compared to scenario one where I had no leveraged debt.

3. *Maximum Leverage.* Now assume that I purchase the same home valued $100,000 and only put down $1,000 as a down payment and finance the remaining $99,000 at 6% ($5,940 annual interest). If the house increases in value by $10,000 in one year, my *rate of return* (appreciation in value) is divided by (the down payment and the interest costs), $10,000 / ($1,000 + $5,940) = 144%! So through leverage of about 100 to 1, I was able to increase my rate of return by triple digits. Picture doing this for several years and as long as values rise, I

would accumulate tens of thousands of dollars on an investment of $1,000 + interest costs. See how this could be so enticing for investors?

Most investment banks were leveraged by a ratio of 30 to 1, and they were dealing with billions of dollars instead of thousands. Government sponsored mortgage giants Freddie (FRE) [the Federal Home Loan Mortgage Corporation] and Fannie were using leverage closer to 100 to 1, because of their supposedly stricter lending standards and implicit government backing. As you know, *when asset prices are rising, this system works like a dream*, but let's look at what happens when asset prices (in this case—houses) move downward.

In scenario #1 above, if the price of the house decreases by $30,000, other than the "paper loss," as long as you don't sell, there are no problems because you have no leveraged debt. In scenario #3 above—maximum leverage, if the price of the house decreases by $30,000, here's what potentially happens:

- Let's assume the bank that lent you the $99,000 decides that the collateral (the value of the house) is no longer sufficient to cover the loan. It may ask you to come up with the difference between the current value of the home ($70,000) and the outstanding debt ($99,000). In order to protect the bank's interests, it will want you to come up with $29,000.

- Now you have two options. First, you can give the bank the $29,000. But you probably didn't have it in the first place, so this is probably not a realistic option. Secondly, you could refinance your mortgage with another bank. But this probably won't work because you already have $29,000 of negative equity. All banks are going to be reluctant to give you money without collateral.

- So you most likely lose the house to foreclosure. This is exactly what is happening to a number of homeowners today.

Now let's map this scenario from a homeowner with a single mortgage to an investment bank that invests in millions of mortgages. If the day you bought the house you had a net worth of $1,000—the cash you put down on your house— then lets say your *personal "stock"* was worth $1,000. After the foreclosure you lost your $1,000 investment and now you personal "stock" is worth $0.

An investment bank may put down $1,000,000 for $30,000,000 worth of mortgages. So lets say the investment bank's stock is worth $1,000,000. As housing prices drop, the investment bank has the same problem as you, they cannot refinance because nobody will lend them more money, so they start losing their houses to foreclosure. As the houses go into foreclosure—one by one—the investment bank's value (and thereby stock) drops. In the end, the investment bank has the same value stock as your personal stock value—zero. Unlike you, the investment banks go hat in hand for a Federal bailout because they failed to manage their downside risk from leveraged debt.

Leverage Needs to Be Understood

So, the lesson of this story is not that leverage is bad; it just has to be understood for both the upside AND downside impacts. If the individual or investment bank were leveraged 3 to 1, they would have enough equity in the house(s) to either refinance or more likely, the bank would not have called in the loan in the first place. Remember if you are leveraged 3 to 1, you have put down 33%. Therefore, the house(s) would have to fall more than 33% to become an issue. Plus, even if the house(s) eventually fell a total of 40% at the market bottom, and the bank called in the loan, you would only need to come up with $7,000 ($67,000 mortgage − $60,000 in current value), which

Excessive Credit, Excessive Risk

We are accustomed to thinking of bubbles and crashes in terms of specific markets—like junk bonds, commercial real estate, and tech stocks. Overpriced assets are like poison mushrooms. You eat them, you get sick, you learn to avoid them.

A credit bubble is different. Credit is the air that financial markets breathe, and when the air is poisoned, there's no place to hide.

Here is a crude gauge of the credit bubble. Not long ago, the sum of all financial assets—stocks, bonds, loans, mortgages, and the like, which are claims on real things— were about equal to global GDP [gross domestic product]. Now they are approaching four times global GDP. Financial derivatives, a form of claim upon financial assets, now have notional values of more than ten times global GDP.

The soaring ratio of credit to real output is a measure of leverage, or financial risk. Think of an inverted pyramid. The more claims are piled on top of real output, the more wobbly the pyramid becomes.

And when large, wobbly objects tumble, they go very fast.

Charles R. Morris,
The Trillion Dollar Meltdown:
Easy Money, High Rollers, and the Great Credit Crash, *2008.*

is much more manageable for an individual or an investment bank than the $39,000 that would be required if you were leveraged 100 to 1 and the house dropped in value by 40%.

Going forward, I hope our regulators take heed of this when the next blend of investment banks emerges and Fannie/

Freddie become profitable again. Hopefully the amount of leverage and actual equity is much more carefully regulated and 30:1 or 100:1 leveraging ratios are banned. Similarly, future homeowners should take this leverage lesson to heart and only purchase homes where they can afford a 20% down payment and so don't get as badly exposed when home prices fall.

Periodical Bibliography

The following articles have been selected to supplement the diverse views presented in this chapter.

Binyamin Appelbaum, Carol D. Leonnig, and David S. Hilzenrath	"How Washington Failed to Rein in Fannie, Freddie," *Washington Post*, September 14, 2008.
Amar Bhide	"In Praise of More Primitive Finance," *Economists' Voice*, February 2009.
William K. Black and Bill Moyers	"Sharing the Blame for the Economic Crisis?" *Bill Moyers Journal*, April 3, 2009.
David Brooks	"Greed and Stupidity," *New York Times*, April 2, 2009.
Jesse Eisinger, Daniel Gross, Duff McDonald, Barry Ritholtz, and Gillian Tett	"Making Sense of the Credit Debacle," *Slate*, March 2–4, 2009.
Thomas Geoghegan	"Infinite Debt: How Unlimited Interest Rates Destroyed the Economy", *Harper's*, April 2009.
Mark Jickling	"Causes of the Financial Crisis," *Congressional Research Services Report for Congress*, January 29, 2009.
Larry Keller	"Minority Meltdown?" *Intelligence Report*, Spring 2009.
Newsweek	"Who's to Blame: Washington or Wall Street?" March 30, 2009.
Bob Ryley	"Blaming the Poor for Wall Street's Mess? The Game Continues," *OpEdNews*, May 25, 2009.
Gary Wolfram	"Accounting Rules at Heart of Bank Crisis," *HumanEvents*, March 13, 2009.

OPPOSING VIEWPOINTS® SERIES

CHAPTER 2

Is the U.S. Banking System in Jeopardy?

Chapter Preface

In 2007, Lehman Brothers stock was trading at $82 a share, its revenues were $19.257 billion, its net profits $4.192 billion, and it employed 28,600 people. In late 2007, it was beginning to be apparent that the company was overly invested in subprime mortgages. By September 2008, Lehman's losses in the mortgage market caused investors to lose confidence in the company, and its stock price and revenues plummeted. When the U.S. government failed to either find a buyer for Lehman or to bail out the company, the 158-year-old business filed for bankruptcy on September 15, 2008, in what would be the largest bankruptcy in U.S. history. The failure of Lehman Brothers was a watershed event that created an erosion of confidence in the U.S. banking system. According to John Garvey, head of the U.S. financial services practice at PricewaterhouseCoopers, the bankruptcy "shook market confidence to its core and caused people to believe the whole system could blow up," as quoted in *USA Today* on September 11, 2009.

The fallout from this failure in confidence was widespread, setting off the most severe financial crisis since the Great Depression. The United States and other advanced economies saw an average 7.5 percent decline in gross domestic product in the fourth quarter of 2008, while developing countries saw a decline of 4 percent. About $14 trillion in household wealth was destroyed as the stock markets plunged and housing prices continued to drop.

By early summer 2008, some economists and politicians were pointing to "green shoots" that indicated the worst of the financial crisis was over and conditions were improving. Martin Neil Baily and Douglas J. Elliott, in a June 2009 Brookings Institution study, "The U.S. Financial and Economic Crisis: Where Does It Stand and Where Do We Go from Here?" pointed to several encouraging signs:

The stock market has now staged a substantial rally and at the end of May [2009] it was nearly 40 percent higher than at its trough in March. The share prices of many financial companies have doubled or more. . . . The rise in share prices has made it feasible for banks to raise capital in the private market and actually pay back some of the TARP [Troubled Asset Relief Program] funds they had taken. The Treasury's stress tests have been completed and most of the banks were pronounced sound and able to withstand even a worsening of the economy from here.

They concluded, "It is possible or even likely that the worst is over in financial markets and the economy will slowly start to mend. However, there are enough risks to this forecast that policymakers and markets cannot relax."

A year after the fall of Lehman Brothers, other analysts considered that the systemic factors leading to the banking crisis had not been addressed, and that the system had not returned to lasting stability. As Alex Berenson stated on September 12, 2009, in the *New York Times*, "The Obama administration has proposed regulatory changes, but even their backers say they face a difficult road in Congress. For now, banks still sell and trade unregulated derivatives, despite their role in last fall's chaos. Radical changes like pay caps or restrictions on bank size face overwhelming resistance. Even minor changes, like requiring banks to disclose more about the derivatives they own, are far from certain." He goes on to say that investors and economists "warn that if the industry's systemic risks are not addressed, they could cause an even bigger crisis."

In the following chapter, the authors weigh in on the question of whether the U.S. banking system has stabilized or still remains in jeopardy.

> *"Almost all [economists] are predicting a turnaround in the third quarter and, and positive growth in the fourth quarter [of 2009]."*

The Economy Is Turning Around

Christina Romer, interviewed by David Gregory

Christina Romer, a U.S. economist, is chair of the president's Council of Economic Advisers and Garff B. Wilson Professor of Economics at the University of California, Berkeley. David Gregory is a U.S. television journalist who moderates the television show Meet the Press.

In the following viewpoint, taken from the transcript of Meet the Press, *Gregory presses Romer on the economic crisis and the Obama administration's assertion that although the economy is currently a mess, the fundamentals of the economy are sound. Gregory challenges her to distinguish between those words and those of Republican senator John McCain, who was roundly criticized for being out of touch when he claimed that the fundamentals of the economy were sound during his presidential campaign. Romer argues that the difference is that today the Obama administration has a plan in place to focus on the fundamentals driving the economy, and the plan is working.*

As you read, consider the following questions:

1. When does Romer believe that the U.S. economy will turn around?

2. Does Romer admit that the U.S. government underestimated the scale of the economic problem?

3. What plans does Romer cite if the current response to the financial crisis is not effective?

*D*avid GREGORY: Billionaire investor Warren Buffett described the economy and the crisis that the economy is in as an economic war. If that's the case, are we winning?

Christina ROMER: I think he's absolutely right, it is an economic war. We have inherited a crisis like none since we've—since we had the Great Depression. So absolutely, it is something we need to deal with. I think we are. We haven't won yet. We have staged a wonderful battle. So we have put in place just a host of programs: the stimulus package, the financial rescue plan, the housing plan. We think it's the right medicine and we think it will work.

President Focusing on Fundamentals

GREGORY: There's an effort across the administration to sound more confident about the economy. The president, speaking on Friday, said this:

(Videotape, Friday)

Barack OBAMA: If we are keeping focused on all the fundamentally sound aspects of our economy, then we're going to get through this. And I'm very confident about that.

(End videotape)

GREGORY: And yet last year during the campaign, Senator John McCain said something similar. This is what he said back then.

(Videotape, September 15, 2008)

JOHN McCAIN: You know that there's been tremendous turmoil in our financial markets and Wall Street, and it is—it's—people are frightened by these events. Our economy, I think—still, the fundamentals our—of our economy are strong, but these are very, very difficult times.

(End videotape)

GREGORY: So back then during the campaign when Senator McCain talked about the strong fundamentals of the economy, it was then-candidate Obama and his team that roundly criticized McCain, saying he was out of touch, he didn't get it, he didn't understand how bad the economy was. And yet now the president's talking about the strong fundamentals of the economy. So what's different between then, the campaign, and now, except for the fact that the economy's gotten dramatically worse?

ROMER: I think when the president says he's focusing on fundamentals, what he means is, is we're focusing on, on fixing the fundamentals; that we've always said we're not looking at the ups and downs of the stock market, we're looking for those crucial indicators: when are jobs turning around, when are sales turning around, when do we see consumers coming to life? That's the kind of thing that—certainly that I'm looking at in terms of when's the economy going to be doing better and, and when can we see some hope.

GREGORY: Are the fundamentals of this economy sound?

ROMER: Well, of course the fundamentals are sound in the sense that the American workers are sound, we have a good capital stock, we have good technology. We know that, that temporarily we're in a mess, right? We've seen huge job loss, we've seen very large falls in GDP [gross domestic product]. So certainly in the short run we're in a, in a bad situation.

GREGORY: All right, but then what's different between now and then, when the economy was in even better shape than it, it is now, when McCain was saying the fundamentals were strong and then-candidate Obama criticized him?

ROMER: I think—again, I think what, what we're saying is that the, you know, where we are today is obviously not good. We have a plan in place to get to a good place. I think that's the crucial—a fundamentally crucial difference, is to make sure that you have put in place all of the comprehensive programs that'll get us back to those fundamentals.

The other thing I think is so important, the president has actually said in terms of fundamentals, we need to make changes. That's why he's focusing on energy, education, getting the budget deficit under control, precisely because he said . . .

GREGORY: Right.

ROMER: . . . when we get through this thing, we want to be in a better place.

GREGORY: But perhaps Senator McCain was right when he said the fundamentals of the economy were strong, because you have President Obama saying roughly the same thing now?

ROMER: I really think you're misinterpreting the president. I think the key thing that the president was saying is we have our eyes on the fundamentals, that is what we're concerned about.

GREGORY: Hmm.

ROMER: And he was—I think very much has been drawing this distinction between the day-to-day ups and downs in the stock market, because that, we know, is a, a bad way, to gauge policy.

Economy Will Turn Around

GREGORY: I want to talk about projections for the economy, where you see it going. You were asked on March 6th that very question, and this is how you responded.

(Videotape, March 6, 2009)

"We are on the road to recovery. We just happen to be going against traffic."

'We are on the road to recovery. We just happen to be going against the traffic.' Cartoon by Ron Morgan.

ROMER: Most people are predicting some time in the second half of the year, and, and I expect that's when we'll start to see positive GDP growth again. And a little after that we'll start to see employment going up rather than going down.

(End videotape)

GREGORY: Pretty strong prediction. What if you're wrong? What's plan B?

ROMER: Well, so one thing—I mean, I should say my prediction is very much what most private forecasters are saying. We know that this last week [of March 15, 2009,] the blue chip economic indicators came out that surveys lots of private forecasters. Almost all of them are predicting a turnaround in the third quarter and, and positive growth in the fourth quarter. Obviously I'm not a fortune teller and, you know, we're going to be watching this thing like a hawk. We've—we think we've put in place the right programs that will bring this kind of a change about, but the president has always said we'll do whatever it takes if it doesn't work.

GREGORY: Well, would you disagree with the notion that government has fundamentally underestimated the scale of this problem going back to the previous administration?

ROMER: I think, I think everybody underestimated the scale of this problem. I think inherently it, it surprised us.

GREGORY: Right.

ROMER: That's why . . .

GREGORY: So if that's the case, there's pretty high probability that even your own prediction will fall short. Which leads to the question then, what's plan B? Don't Americans deserve to know what the administration is thinking about doing if those projects don't, don't bear out?

ROMER: Well, there are a couple of things. One is that as—you know, as this has gone on, we're getting lots more information. So the chances that we're going to be surprised, I think, are going down. You know, I think the, the crucial thing, you know, we have put in place what is, is just simply the biggest, boldest recovery package in history, right; the stimulus package, biggest ever; the financial rescue, absolutely comprehensive; a housing plan—that is incredible medicine for the economy. And we fully expect it to work. That's why we put those, those policies in place.

> *"The storm is not over, not by a long shot. Huge structural flaws remain in the architecture of our financial system."*

The Economy Will Not Turn Around Until Structural Flaws Are Fixed

Sandy B. Lewis and William D. Cohan

Sandy B. Lewis is the founder of S.B. Lewis & Company, a brokerage house. He pled guilty to three charges of stock manipulation in 1989, was pardoned by President Bill Clinton in 2001, and had his lifetime ban on trading overturned by the Securities and Exchange Commission in 2006. He is currently an organic farmer. William D. Cohan is a former investigative reporter who spent seventeen years on Wall Street, his last years as a managing director at JPMorgan Chase. He writes frequently for the Daily Beast, Fortune, *and the* Financial Times *and is the author of* House of Cards: A Tale of Hubris and Wretched Excess on Wall Street.

The Obama administration's solutions to the banking crisis simply address the symptoms of the crisis without getting to its

*fundamental roots, claim Lewis and Cohan in the following ex-
cerpt. Instead of attempting to fix the present system, the authors
argue, the administration should construct a new system. This
new system should incorporate a compensation system that rewards prudent risk and holds bankers accountable for failure
and provides greater transparency for investors about what is oc-
curring in the financial markets.*

As you read, consider the following questions:

1. What changes to the compensation system for bankers
   do the authors recommend?

2. What experience do Lewis and Cohan recommend economic advisors have?

3. What do the authors believe should be the purpose of
   their recommended hearing on the cause of the crisis?

Whether at a fund-raising dinner for wealthy supporters
in Beverly Hills, or at an Air Force base in Nevada, or
at [broadcast journalist] Charlie Rose's table in New York City,
President [Barack] Obama is conducting an all-out campaign
to try to make us feel a whole lot better about the economy as
quickly as possible. "It's safe to say we have stepped back from
the brink, that there is some calm that didn't exist before," he
told donors at the Beverly Hilton Hotel late [in May 2009].

Mr. Obama thinks that the way to revive the economy is
to restore confidence in it. If the mood is right, the capital
will flow. But this belief is dangerously misguided. We are
sympathetic to the extraordinary challenge the president faces,
but if we've learned anything at all two years into the worst financial crisis of our lifetimes, it is that a capital-markets system this dependent on public confidence is a shockingly inadequate foundation upon which to rest our economy.

We have both spent large chunks of our lives working on
Wall Street, absorbing its ethic and mores. We're concerned
that nothing has really been fixed. . . .

Flaws Must Be Fixed

The storm is not over, not by a long shot. Huge structural flaws remain in the architecture of our financial system, and many of the fixes that the Obama administration has proposed will do little to address them and may make them worse. At another fund-raising event, for Senator Harry Reid, President Obama said: "We didn't ask for the challenges that we face. But we are determined to answer the call to meet those challenges, to cast aside the old arguments and overcome the stubborn divisions and move forward as one people and one nation. . . . It will take time but I promise you, I promise you, I'll always tell you the truth about the challenges we face."

Keeping that statement in mind—as well as an abiding faith in the importance of properly functioning capital markets—we have come up with a set of questions meant to challenge a popular president, with vast majorities in Congress, to find the flaws in the system, to figure out what's being done to fix them and to get to the truth about the difficulties we face as we set out to restore the proper functioning of our markets and our standing in the world.

[At the beginning of 2009], nobody believed that our banking system was well designed, functioning smoothly or properly regulated—so why then are we so desperately anxious to restore that model as the status quo? Nearly every new program emanating these days from the Treasury Department—the Term Asset-Backed Securities Loan Facility, the Public Private Investment Program, the "stress tests" of major banks—appears to have been designed to either paper over or to prop up a system that has clearly failed.

Instead of hauling out the new drywall to cover up the existing studs, let's seriously consider ripping down the entire structure, dynamiting the foundation and building a new system that rewards taking prudent risks, allocates capital where it is needed, allows all investors to get accurate and timely financial information and increases value to shareholders and creditors.

As a start, the best-compensated executives at the top of these big banks, hedge funds[1] and private-equity firms[2] should be treated like general partners of yore. If a firm takes prudent risks that pay off, this top layer of management should be well compensated. But if the risks these people take are imprudent and the losses grave, they should expect to lose their jobs. Instead of getting guaranteed salaries or huge bonuses, they should have the bulk of their net worth completely at risk for a long stretch of time—10 years come to mind—for the decisions they make while in charge. This would go a long way toward re-aligning the interests of these firms with those of their shareholders and clients and the American people, who have been saddled with their risks and mistakes. . . .

Bank Bailouts Must Stop

Why is the morphine drip still in the veins of the financial system? These trillions in profligate [wasteful] federal spending are intended to make us feel better again even though feeling pain, and dealing with it responsibly, would be healthier in the long run. It is time to stop rescuing the banks that got us into this mess. If that means more bank failures on a grander scale or the dismemberment of Citigroup, so be it. Depositors will be protected—up to $250,000 per account—but shareholders, creditors and, sadly, many employees will, for the long-term health of the system, need to feel the market's wrath. . . .

Furthermore, for government leaders to decide who shall live and who shall die in an economic sense opens them up to

1. A hedge fund is a pooled private investment fund that seeks to maximize returns with strategies that include unconventional investments and investments that cannot easily be converted to cash, such as real estate.
2. Private-equity firms raise funds that are then invested in securities or by buying companies.

Collapse of a System

There are two features that I think deserve to be pointed out. One is that the financial system as we know it actually collapsed. After the bankruptcy of Lehman Brothers on September 15, [2009,] the financial system really ceased to function. It had to be put on artificial life support. At the same time, the financial shock had a tremendous effect on the real economy, and the real economy went into a free fall, and that was global.

The other feature is that the financial system collapsed of its own weight. That contradicted the prevailing view about financial markets, namely that they tend toward equilibrium, and that equilibrium is disturbed by extraneous forces, outside shocks. Those disturbances were supposed to occur in a random fashion. Markets were seen basically as self-correcting. That paradigm has proven to be false. So we are dealing not only with the collapse of a financial system, but also with the collapse of a worldview.

George Soros, New York Review of Books, June 11, 2009.

legitimate charges of crony capitalism and favoritism. We will benefit in the long run from a return to market discipline.

Traders Should Become Advisers

Why has Mr. Obama surrounded himself largely with economic advisers who are theoreticians and academics—distinguished though they may be—but not those who have sat on a trading desk, made a market, managed a portfolio or set a spread?

In our view, one of the ways out of this economic conundrum is to have experienced traders—not hothouse flowers—

design incentives that will encourage the market to have buyers and sellers meet anew around the proper valuations of assets, not some artificial construct of a market propped up by a pliant Financial Accounting Standards Board or government-sponsored programs that appear to be virtually giving money away to hedge funds and private-equity firms so that they will buy assets they would not ordinarily buy. We're not talking about putting the fox in charge of the henhouse, just putting people who know how markets function in the real world into the important seats in Washington.

More Information Made Public

Why isn't the Obama administration working night and day to give the public a vastly increased amount of detailed information about what happens in financial markets? Ever since traders started disappearing from the floor of the New York Stock Exchange in the last decade of the 20th century, there has been less and less transparency about the price and volume of trades. The New York Stock Exchange really exists in name only, as computers execute a very large percentage of all trades, far away from any exchange.

As a result, there is little flow of information, and small investors are paying the price. The beneficiaries, no surprise, are the remains of the old Wall Street broker-dealers—now bank-holding companies like Goldman Sachs and Morgan Stanley—that can see in advance what their clients are interested in buying, and might trade the same stocks for their own accounts. Incredibly, despite the events of [late 2008], nearly every one of Wall Street's proprietary trading desks can still take huge risks and then, if they get into trouble, head to the Federal Reserve for short-term rescue financing.

Here's something that should change in terms of transparency. The most recent price that any stock traded for should be published online in real time for all to see. And the public should have access to a new type of electronic ticker that provides market information in language that all can understand, not just the insiders.

As for those impossibly complex securities that caused so much of the trouble—among them derivatives, credit-default swaps and asset-backed securities—the S.E.C. [Securities and Exchange Commission] should have the power to make public all the documentation surrounding these weapons of mass financial destruction, including all data about the current costs of buying and selling them and the cash flow underlying them. We also need widely accessible, real-time reporting of all trades in the bond market. We bet Mike Bloomberg's company [an information and software provider to the financial community] could help design such a system for our benefit.

Why is the government still complicit in making the system ever less transparent, even when it comes to what should clearly be considered public information? For instance, it took more than a year for the Federal Reserve to disclose that it had agreed to pay BlackRock—the huge money manager that is 45 percent owned by Bank of America—and others $71 million in a no-bid contract to manage the $30 billion of toxic assets that JPMorgan did not want when it bought Bear Stearns in March 2008. And that is only one of the five contracts BlackRock has with the government as a result of this crisis—the nature of the other contracts remains secret. . . .

Preventing Repeats

Why hasn't President Obama insisted on public hearings over what happened during this financial crisis?

Not a single top executive of a Wall Street securities firm responsible for causing the financial crisis has had the courage or the decency to step forward in front of the cameras and explain to the American people in his own words exactly how and why he allowed his firm to cause the crisis. Both Mr. [Richard] Fuld [of Lehman Bros.] and Alan Schwartz, the chief executive of Bear Stearns at the end, in their Congressional testimony blamed the proverbial once-in-a-century financial tsunami. Do they or any of their peers really think this is true?

There may be a way to find out. There is much talk nowadays coming from top bankers—Lloyd Blankfein of Goldman Sachs, Jamie Dimon of JPMorganChase, John Mack of Morgan Stanley and even Ken Lewis of Bank of America—about seeing how quickly they can repay to the Treasury the TARP [Troubled Asset Relief Program] money Mr. [Henry] Paulson [secretary of the treasury] forced on them. One precondition of their being allowed to repay the funds should be a requirement that each gives a public deposition and explains, under oath, what truly happened and why.

Such a public hearing would be meant only to offer a truthful assessment of the errors in judgment made at each firm and to promote understanding, so that we—somehow—can avoid repeating the same mistakes again. It would not be about indictments. These men should be offered use immunity from prosecution for their honest testimony, but only with a clear understanding that the failure to tell the truth at any point would result in serious legal consequences. The hearing could be complemented by a truth-seeking commission established to hear the accounts of several people who have departed the scene, including, among others, Mr. Paulson, former Treasury Secretary Robert Rubin and former Wall Street chiefs like Mr. Fuld, Hank Greenberg of A.I.G., Sanford Weill of Citigroup, Jimmy Cayne of Bear Stearns and Stan O'Neal of Merrill Lynch. While far removed from their positions of authority, these men have tales to tell about how this crisis got started and why. . . .

We are in one of those "generational revolutions" that [Thomas] Jefferson said were as important as anything else to the proper functioning of our democracy. We can no longer pretend that our collective behavior as a nation for the past 25 years has been worthy of us as a people. Many of us hoped that Barack Obama's election would redress the dire decline in our collective ethic. We are 139 days into his presidency, and while there is still plenty of hope that Mr. Obama will fulfill his mandate, his record on searching out the causes of the financial crisis has not been reassuring. He must do what is necessary to restore the American people's—and the world's—faith in American capitalism and in our nation. Answering our questions may help us get back on track. But time is wasting.

"We must provide banks with the capital and the confidence necessary to start lending again."

Bailouts Are Necessary to Restore the Banking System

Barack Obama

Barack Obama is the forty-fourth president of the United States.

In the following excerpt, President Obama explains the causes of the financial crisis and defends his administration's actions in responding to the crisis. He describes a "perfect storm" of risk-taking that began with homeowners buying houses they couldn't afford and investment banks packaging those risky mortgages and selling them to investors. When the housing bubble collapsed, the value of these mortgages and investments dropped and banks found themselves left with debt they could not pay off. This resulted in banks being unwilling and unable to lend money, and it had a devastating effect on the economy. In order to get banks lending money again, it was necessary for the U.S. government to provide them with financial assistance, Obama argues.

Barack Obama, "A New Foundation for the Economy," speech at Georgetown University, April 14, 2009.

As you read, consider the following questions:

1. In Obama's opinion, how did what happened on Wall Street permeate the entire U.S. economy?

2. What first step does the president describe his administration as taking to address the financial crisis?

3. What are the "five pillars" that Obama cites that will rebuild the U.S. economy?

Recessions are not uncommon. Markets and economies naturally ebb and flow, as we have seen many times in our history. But this recession is different. This recession was not caused by a normal downturn in the business cycle. It was caused by a perfect storm of irresponsibility and poor decision-making that stretched from Wall Street to Washington to Main Street.

How We Got Here

As has been widely reported, it started in the housing market. During the course of the decade, the formula for buying a house changed: instead of saving their pennies to buy their dream house, many Americans found they could take out loans that by traditional standards their incomes just could not support. Others were tricked into signing these subprime loans by lenders who were trying to make a quick profit. And the reason these loans were so readily available was that Wall Street saw big profits to be made. Investment banks would buy and package together these questionable mortgages into securities,[1] arguing that by pooling the mortgages, the risks had been reduced. And credit agencies that are supposed to help investors determine the soundness of various investments stamped the securities with their safest rating when they should have been labeled "Buyer Beware."

1. Securities are investment instruments issued by a government or corporation representing financial value in that entity.

No one really knew what the actual value of these securities were, but since the housing market was booming and prices were rising, banks and investors kept buying and selling them, always passing off the risk to someone else for a greater profit without having to take any of the responsibility. Banks took on more debt than they could handle. The government-chartered companies Fannie Mae [Federal National Mortgage Association] and Freddie Mac [Federal Home Loan Mortgage Corporation], whose traditional mandate was to help support traditional mortgages, decided to get in on the action by buying and holding billions of dollars of these securities. AIG, the biggest insurer in the world, decided to make profits by selling billions of dollars of complicated financial instruments that supposedly insured these securities. Everybody was making record profits—except the wealth created was real only on paper. And as the bubble grew, there was almost no accountability or oversight from anyone in Washington.

Then the housing bubble burst. Home prices fell. People began defaulting on their subprime mortgages. The value of all those loans and securities plummeted. Banks and investors couldn't find anyone to buy them. Greed gave way to fear. Investors pulled their money out of the market. Large financial institutions that didn't have enough money on hand to pay off all their obligations collapsed. Other banks held on tight to the money they did have and simply stopped lending.

This is when the crisis spread from Wall Street to Main Street. After all, the ability to get a loan is how you finance the purchase of everything from a home to a car to a college education. It's how stores stock their shelves, farms buy equipment, and businesses make payroll. So when banks stopped lending money, businesses started laying off workers. When laid off workers had less money to spend, businesses were forced to lay off even more workers. When people couldn't get car loans, a bad situation at the auto companies became even worse. When people couldn't get home loans, the crisis in the housing market only deepened. Because the infected securities were being traded worldwide and other nations also had weak regulations, this recession soon became global. And when other nations can't afford to buy our goods, it slows our economy even further.

The Recovery Plan

This is the situation we confronted on the day we took office. And so our most urgent task has been to clear away the wreckage, repair the immediate damage to the economy, and do everything we can to prevent a larger collapse. And since the problems we face are all working off each other to feed a vicious economic downturn, we've had no choice but to attack all fronts of our economic crisis at once.

The first step was to fight a severe shortage of demand in the economy. The Federal Reserve did this by dramatically lowering interest rates [in 2008] in order to boost investment. And my administration and Congress boosted demand by passing the largest recovery plan in our nation's history. It's a plan that is already in the process of saving or creating 3.5 million jobs over the next two years. It is putting money directly in people's pockets with a tax cut for 95% of working families that is now showing up in paychecks across America. And to cushion the blow of this recession, we also provided extended unemployment benefits and continued health care coverage to Americans who have lost their jobs through no fault of their own.

Now, some have argued that this recovery plan is a case of irresponsible government spending; that it is somehow to blame for our long-term deficit projections, and that the federal government should be cutting instead of increasing spending right now. So let me tackle this argument head on.

To begin with, economists on both the left and right agree that the last thing a government should do in the middle of a recession is to cut back on spending. You see, when this recession began, many families sat around their kitchen table and tried to figure out where they could cut back. So do many businesses. That is a completely responsible and understandable reaction. But if every family in America cuts back, then no one is spending any money, which means there are more layoffs, and the economy gets even worse. That's why the government has to step in and temporarily boost spending in order to stimulate demand. And that's exactly what we're doing right now.

Second of all, I absolutely agree that our long-term deficit is a major problem that we have to fix. But the fact is that this recovery plan represents only a tiny fraction of that long-term deficit. As I will discuss in a moment, the key to dealing with our deficit and debt is to get a handle on out-of-control health care costs—not to stand idly by as the economy goes into free fall.

So the recovery plan has been the first step in confronting this economic crisis. The second step has been to heal our financial system so that credit is once again flowing to the businesses and families who rely on it.

The heart of this financial crisis is that too many banks and other financial institutions simply stopped lending money. In a climate of fear, banks were unable to replace their losses by raising new capital on their own, and they were unwilling to lend the money they did have because they were afraid that no one would pay it back. It is for this reason that the last administration used the Troubled Asset Relief Program, or TARP, to provide these banks with temporary financial assistance in order to get them lending again.

Now, I don't agree with some of the ways the TARP program was managed, but I do agree with the broader rationale that we must provide banks with the capital and the confidence necessary to start lending again. That is the purpose of the stress tests that will soon tell us how much additional capital will be needed to support lending at our largest banks.

Public Supports Government Investment to Secure U.S. Financial System

	Total	Rep	Dem	Ind
Gov't plan is the...	%	%	%	%
Right thing to do	57	64	56	54
Wrong thing to do	30	28	29	32
Don't know/Refused	13	8	15	14
	100	100	100	100

Question wording: "As you may know, the government is potentially investing billions to try and keep financial institutions and markets secure. Do you think this is the right thing or the wrong thing for the government to be doing?"

TAKEN FROM: Pew Research Center for the People & the Press, "Public Supports Government Investment to Secure U.S. Financial System," September 23, 2008.

Ideally, these needs will be met by private investors. But where this is not possible, and banks require substantial additional resources from the government, we will hold accountable those responsible, force the necessary adjustments, provide the support to clean up their balance sheets, and assure the continuity of a strong, viable institution that can serve our people and our economy.

Of course, there are some who argue that the government should stand back and simply let these banks fail—especially since in many cases it was their bad decisions that helped create the crisis in the first place. But whether we like it or not, history has repeatedly shown that when nations do not take early and aggressive action to get credit flowing again, they have crises that last years and years instead of months and months—years of low growth, low job creation, and low investment that cost those nations far more than a course of bold, upfront action. And although there are a lot of Americans who understandably think that government money would be better spent going directly to families and businesses instead of banks—"where's our bailout?" they ask—the truth is that a dollar of capital in a bank can actually result in eight or ten dollars of loans to families and businesses, a multiplier effect that can ultimately lead to a faster pace of economic growth.

On the other hand, there have been some who don't dispute that we need to shore up the banking system, but suggest that we have been too timid in how we go about it. They say that the federal government should have already preemptively stepped in and taken over major financial institutions the way that the FDIC [Federal Deposit Insurance Corporation] currently intervenes in smaller banks, and that our failure to do so is yet another example of Washington coddling Wall Street. So let me be clear—the reason we have not taken this step has nothing to do with any ideological or political judgment we've made about government involvement in banks, and it's certainly not because of any concern we have for the management and shareholders whose actions have helped cause this mess.

Rather, it is because we believe that preemptive government takeovers are likely to end up costing taxpayers even more in the end, and because it is more likely to undermine than to create confidence. Governments should practice the same principle as doctors: first do no harm. So rest assured—we will do whatever is necessary to get credit flowing again, but we will do so in ways that minimize risks to taxpayers and to the broader economy. To that end, in addition to the program to provide capital to the banks, we have launched a plan that will pair government resources with private investment in order to clear away the old loans and securities—the so-called toxic assets—that are also preventing our banks from lending money. . . .

Preventing Another Crisis

But even as we continue to clear away the wreckage and address the immediate crisis, it is my firm belief that our next task is to make sure such a crisis never happens again. Even as we clean up balance sheets and get credit flowing; even as people start spending and business start hiring—we have to realize that we cannot go back to the bubble and bust economy that led us to this point.

It is simply not sustainable to have a 21st century financial system that is governed by 20th century rules and regulations that allowed the recklessness of a few to threaten the entire economy. It is not sustainable to have an economy where in one year, 40% of our corporate profits came from a financial sector that was based too much on inflated home prices, maxed out credit cards, overleveraged banks and overvalued assets; or an economy where the incomes of the top 1% have skyrocketed while the typical working household has seen their income decline by nearly $2,000.

For even as too many were chasing ever-bigger bonuses and short-term profits over the last decade, we continued to neglect the long-term threats to our prosperity: the crushing burden that the rising cost of health care is placing on families and businesses; the failure of our education system to prepare our workers for a new age; the progress that other nations are making on clean energy industries and technologies while we remain addicted to foreign oil; the growing debt that we're passing on to our children. And even after we emerge from the current recession, these challenges will still represent major obstacles that stand in the way of our success in the 21st century.

There is a parable at the end of the Sermon on the Mount that tells the story of two men. The first built his house on a pile of sand, and it was destroyed as soon as the storm hit. But the second is known as the wise man, for when ". . . the rain descended, and the floods came, and the winds blew, and beat upon that house . . . it fell not: for it was founded upon a rock."

We cannot rebuild this economy on the same pile of sand. We must build our house upon a rock. We must lay a new foundation for growth and prosperity—a foundation that will move us from an era of borrow and spend to one where we save and invest; where we consume less at home and send more exports abroad.

It's a foundation built upon five pillars that will grow our economy and make this new century another American century: new rules for Wall Street that will reward drive and innovation; new investments in education that will make our workforce more skilled and competitive; new investments in renewable energy and technology that will create new jobs and industries; new investments in health care that will cut costs for families and businesses; and new savings in our federal budget that will bring down the debt for future generations. That is the new foundation we must build.

*"The bailout would impose considerable
additional economic damage."*

Bailouts Are Bad
for the Economy

Daniel Mitchell

*Daniel Mitchell is a senior fellow at the Cato Institute, a liber-
tarian think tank, and was formerly a senior fellow at The Heritage Foundation, a conservative think tank.*

*In the following viewpoint, Mitchell finds it ironic that the
same federal government whose policies caused the financial crisis now believes that yet additional federal intervention is needed
to solve these problems. He contends that the bailout of financial
institutions will ultimately hurt the economy. He argues that the
bailout will encourage corruption in the federal government, reward companies that made bad decisions, and encourage risky
behavior in the future.*

As you read, consider the following questions:

1. What are the five reasons the author gives for why bailouts are bad for the country?

Daniel Mitchell, "Why the Bailout Is Bad for America," *Real Clear Politics*, October 1,
2008. Reproduced by permission of the author.

2. In the opinion of Mitchell, what are some of the actions the U.S. government took that created the financial crisis?

3. What reason does the author cite to support his thesis that short-term stock market performance is an unreliable indicator of the efficacy of government monetary policy?

The proposed bailout of the financial system is a misguided scheme that will hurt the U.S. economy in the short run and long run. The economy currently is stumbling as a consequence of a government-created housing bubble, but a bailout of companies, executives, and shareholders that made unwise decisions would, at best, extend the economy's adjustment process. More likely, the bailout would impose considerable additional economic damage because political factors would at least partially supplant market forces in determining the allocation of resources.

Some politicians and government officials are making reckless charges of greater financial turmoil in the absence of a bailout. These grossly irresponsible statements may cause short-term market losses as investors try to second-guess how other investors will respond, but the assertion that the stock market's health—especially in the long run—depends on bigger government is belied by real-world evidence. Japanese politicians made many of the same mistakes in the 1990s that American politicians today are considering, and the Nikkei [a stock market index for the Tokyo Stock Exchange] suffered a lengthy period of decline—and remains today far below its peak level.

Proponents of a bailout also are trying to rattle credit markets by arguing that inaction will cripple commercial and household lending. Fortunately, there is little evidence of a freeze in credit markets, thought the Administration's rash rhetoric and the specter of a bailout doubtlessly are causing needless uncertainty and temporarily higher interest rates. Once the issue is resolved, one way or the other, credit markets will resume normal operations. The only question is whether capital allocation will be distorted—and long-run growth hindered—by government intervention.

Providing government with enormous—and opaque—new powers is likely to exacerbate economic uncertainty and increase system-wide risk. There is no need to incur this additional risk when the Federal Reserve and Federal Deposit Insurance Corporation have been able to deal with several major institution insolvencies (Washington Mutual, Wachovia, Bear-Stearns, Lehman Brothers, and AIG) with existing authority.

Why the Bailout Is Bad

The bailout is bad for the economy. The unfortunate truth is that bad government policy has resulted in excess investment in the housing sector, and the inevitable reallocation of labor and capital is going to cause some economic dislocation. The good news, though, is that this process—if not hindered—will create a stronger and more vibrant economy. A bailout, however, will discourage this process and reduce economic efficiency. This may not seem important in the short run, since modest changes in the rate of economic growth are difficult to perceive. But in the long run, because of compounding, even small changes in the rate of growth can have a significant impact on living standards. Small differences in annual growth rates are why disposable income in the United States is substantially higher than disposable income in nations that practice economic interventionism, such as France, Germany, and Japan.

The bailout repeats the mistakes Japan made in the 1990s. There are several historical episodes that indicate the dangers of government intervention to prop up a bubble. Japan faced a similar situation at the end of the 1980s, with real estate prices rising to absurd levels. The bubble then burst, but rather than let market forces operate, Japanese politicians sought to prop up both insolvent institution and asset prices. This interfered with the orderly reallocation of labor and capital, created considerable uncertainty, and contributed to a "lost decade" of economic stagnation. Another worrisome parallel is what happened during the 1930s. Policy mistakes such as protectionism (Hoover), higher tax rates (Hoover and Roosevelt), increased government spending (Hoover and Roosevelt) and increased intervention (Hoover and Roosevelt), helped turn a stock-market correction into the Great Depression.

The bailout will increase corruption in Washington. When politicians have more power over the allocation of economic resources, people have an incentive to play the "rent-seeking" game of exchanging campaign contributions and hiring lobbyists in hopes of obtaining unearned wealth (or, more honorably, taking the same steps in hopes of protecting themselves from those seeking unearned wealth). The squalid mess at Fannie Mae [the Federal National Mortgage Association] and Freddie Mac [the Federal Home Loan Mortgage Corporation] was made possible in part because politicians received enormous amounts of money from advocates of the two government-sponsored enterprises. If the government obtains power over financial markets, including the ability to steer money to particular firms, it will create a feeding frenzy of lobbying and influence peddling.

The bailout rewards executives and companies that made poor choices. Unfettered markets are the best generator of prosperity because people have incentives to make wise decisions. If an entrepreneur figures out a way to provide a valued good or service to others, he can become wealthy. But if that entrepreneur makes a mistake, he will suffer losses and maybe even bankruptcy. If investors put money into a well-run company, they can increase their wealth. But if they put their money into a poorly-run firm, the opposite can happen. In other words, market forces encourage people to make smart

decisions so they can prosper. But it is equally important that people bear the consequences when they make wrong choices.

The bailout will encourage imprudent risk in the future. The debacles at Fannie Mae and Freddie Mac, as well as the savings and loan failures from the late 1980s/early 1990s, are compelling examples of the negative economic consequences that occur when profits are privatized but losses are socialized. Faced with this perverse incentive structure, people engage in riskier behavior (analogously, if you are in Vegas, and somebody else is going to cover your losses, you obviously have an incentive to make bigger bets). A bailout would extend this risky behavior to the whole financial system, if not the entire economy.

Government-Caused Turmoil

One of the ironies of the bailout debate is that supporters think that more government intervention is the solution to problems caused by bad government policy. The main mistake was probably the Federal Reserve's easy-money policy. By creating too much liquidity and by driving interest rates to artificially low levels, the Fed set in motion the conditions for a housing bubble.

But this housing bubble is particularly severe because another government mistake—the pernicious and corrupt policies of Fannie Mae and Freddie Mac—lured many people into mortgages that they could not afford. When a housing bubble bursts, that can have a negative effect on economic activity because people lose wealth (or lose the perception of wealth). But when people have been lured into homes they cannot afford and a bubble bursts, the economic consequences are more severe when a bubble bursts because people not only lose wealth, they also lose their homes.

Other mistakes include policies such as the Community Reinvestment Act, which extorted banks into making loans to consumers with poor credit. There are also many other policies that have encouraged economically inefficient levels of housing investment, such as the mortgage interest deduction in the tax code.

An Odd Benchmark

Supporters of the bailout breathlessly watch the Dow Jones Industrial Average and interpret any downward movement as evidence that a bailout is necessary. This is a rather odd benchmark, particularly since it almost goes without saying that a $700 billion transfer from taxpayers to the financial industry is going to increase—at least in the short run—the value of financial assets. A $700 billion transfer from taxpayers to the auto industry would increase the value of auto companies, but that is hardly an argument for such a handout.

Moreover, short-term stock market performance is a bad indicator of good government policy. The Dow Jones Industrial Average rose substantially in the weeks following the imposition of wage and price controls by Richard Nixon in 1971. Yet Nixon's policy caused considerable economic damage by hindering market forces. And since it did not address the real cause of rising prices—an easy-money policy by the Federal Reserve, Nixon let the problem fester and worsen, which un-avoidably was a major reason for the relatively deep economic recession in 1974–75.

One of the reasons why short-term stock market perfor-mance can be misleading is that investors sometimes care more about what other investors think than they do about the underlying fundamentals. This is known as the "Keynesian[1] beauty contest," and though it is not a sound approach for long-term investing, it a perfectly reasonable strategy for speculative short-term investments. And in today's volatile en-vironment—particularly with the reckless comments by Ad-ministration officials and Members of Congress, many inves-tors will assume lower stock prices because they think other investors assume lower stock prices.

When government tries to redistribute wealth from rich people to poor people, it causes economic damage by discour-aging productive activity by the most successful and by dis-couraging productive activity from those who are lured into government dependency. The proposed bailout is even more pernicious. It would redistribute wealth from poor people to rich people, and simultaneously encourage reckless behavior by recipients and impose an immoral burden on those that behaved responsibly.

1. John Maynard Keynes was a British economist who advocated roles for both the pri-vate sector and government in the economy and whose theories were widely accepted and followed.

> "The potentially devastating effects on confidence, financial markets, and the broader economy that would likely arise from the . . . failure of a major financial firm . . . [are] extremely serious."

Some Banks Are Too Big to Let Fail

Ben S. Bernanke

Ben S. Bernanke is chairman of the board of governors of the U.S. Federal Reserve Bank. He has served as director of Monetary Economics Projects of the National Bureau of Economic Research and as editor of American Economic Review. *He was named the fourth most powerful person in the world in 2008 by* Newsweek *magazine.*

In the following viewpoint taken from a speech Bernanke made to a group of community bankers, he argues that some banks are too big to let fail. While acknowledging the frustration that community bankers may feel by the bailout of large institutions whose risky behavior caused the crisis, Bernanke points to the devastating effect the failure of a major institution would have on the financial system.

Ben S. Bernanke, "The Financial Crisis and Community Banking," speech at the Independent Community Bankers of America's National Convention and Techworld, March 20, 2009.

As you read, consider the following questions:

1. What are the two steps that the author states need to be taken to improve the financial regulatory system?

2. What are the five actions that Bernanke recommends policy makers take to address the too-big-to-fail issue?

3. What are steps that the author tells community bankers that they can take to safeguard their institutions?

When I addressed this convention three years ago [in 2006], with all of five weeks under my belt as Chairman of the Federal Reserve Board, I opened my remarks with three observations: that community banks played a critical role in the U.S. economy, that community banks were generally doing well, and that community banks faced a changing business environment that posed important challenges. I am struck that all three observations, at least to some degree, still hold true today. Community banks continue to play a critical role in our economy and, in many cases, have an opportunity to step in and make sound profitable loans, where some competitors have pulled back. Relatively speaking at least, community banks are doing better as a group than other segments of our financial system, but at the same time they are far from immune to current conditions. And, surely, it is still true that the business environment poses important challenges to community banks.

In fact, I think it is safe to say that few of us in the convention hall three years ago envisioned the financial and economic environment we now confront. Envisioning the conditions we will face three years from now is equally difficult, but it is my hope and expectation that those conditions will be significantly brighter. . . . I'll discuss two important steps that policymakers can and should take to improve the financial regulatory system that likely are of particular interest to you. The first step is the need to address the very real problem

Making Too-Big-to-Fail Banks Safer

A strong case can be made for creating incentives that reduce the size and complexity of financial institutions as being bigger is not necessarily better. A financial system characterized by a handful of giant institutions with global reach and a single regulator is making a huge bet that those few banks and their regulator over a long period of time will always make the right decisions at the right time.

Reliance solely on the supervision of these institutions is not enough. We also need a "fail-safe" system where if any one large institution fails, the system carries on without breaking down. Financial firms that pose systemic risks should be subject to regulatory and economic incentives that require these institutions to hold larger capital and liquidity buffers to mirror the heightened risk they pose to the financial system.

Sheila C. Bair, Statement to Senate Committee
on Banking, Housing and Urban Affairs, May 6, 2009.

caused by institutions that are too big—or too interconnected—to fail in a disorderly manner. The second involves ways of making the system less procyclical,[1] so that the financial system is less susceptible to exuberant booms and disastrous busts. In discussing the road back to financial stability and economic prosperity, I want to leave you with the idea that, yes, this is indeed a time of challenge for community bankers, as it is for all Americans, but it also is a time of opportunity. . . .

---

1. A procyclical system is one in which there is a direct, positive correlation between an event and the state of the economy. That is, any quantity that tends to increase when the overall economy is growing is classified as procyclical.

The Too-Big-to-Fail Problem

Many of you likely are frustrated, and rightfully so, by the impact that the financial crisis and economic downturn has had on your banks, as well as on the reputation of bankers more generally. You may well have built your reputations and institutions through responsible lending and community-focused operations, but nonetheless, you now find yourselves facing higher deposit insurance assessments and increasing public skepticism about the behavior of bankers—outcomes that you perceive were largely caused by the actions of larger financial institutions. Many of you managed your businesses prudently and shunned more exotic instruments and activities. And many of your customers—households and businesses—avoided excesses and are able to meet their financial commitments on a timely basis.

No doubt this frustration has been heightened by the problems caused by financial firms that are too big or too interconnected to fail. Indeed, the too-big-to-fail issue has emerged as an enormous problem, both for policymakers and for financial institutions generally. Creditors of a firm perceived as too big to fail have less incentive to monitor and restrict the firm's risk-taking through adjustments to the price at which they lend money to the firm. If left unaddressed, this weakening of market discipline creates an unlevel playing field for smaller institutions, which may not be able to raise funds as cheaply, even if their individual risk profiles are better, or at least no worse, than those of their larger competitors. The erosion in market discipline distorts market behavior and can give firms an incentive to grow—either internally or through acquisitions—in order to be perceived as too big to fail.

Government rescues to prevent the failure of major financial institutions also have required large amounts of public resources. These actions have involved extremely unpleasant and difficult choices, but given the interconnected nature of our financial system and the potentially devastating effects on confidence, financial markets, and the broader economy that would likely arise from the disorderly failure of a major financial firm in the current environment, I do not think we have had a realistic alternative to preventing such failures. That said, these episodes have shown clearly that the problem of too-big-to-fail is extremely serious. To address this issue, which should be a top priority for financial reform, policymakers will need to act on several fronts.

First, supervisors—as we are already doing—must vigorously address the weaknesses at major financial institutions with regard to capital adequacy, liquidity management, and risk management. Firms whose failure would pose a systemic risk must receive especially close supervisory oversight and be held to the highest prudential standards. Aside from its direct benefits for the safety and soundness of these large institutions, such an approach also would help offset financial firms' incentive to grow until they are perceived to be too big to fail.

Second, supervisors must pay close attention to compensation practices that can create mismatches between the rewards and risks borne by institutions or their managers. As the Federal Reserve and other banking agencies have noted, poorly designed compensation policies can create perverse incentives that can ultimately jeopardize the health of the banking organization. Management compensation policies should be aligned with the long-term prudential interests of the institution, be tied to the risks being borne by the organization, provide appropriate incentives for safe and sound behavior, and avoid short-term payments for transactions with long-term horizons.

Third, as the recent financial crisis has highlighted, risks to the financial system may arise not only in the banking sector, but also from financial firms that traditionally have been outside the regulatory and supervisory framework applied to banking organizations. Under federal law, all banking organizations—regardless of size—are subject to consolidated supervision for safety and soundness purposes. At a minimum, policymakers must ensure that a similar statutory framework is put in place for all systemically important financial firms organized as holding companies. The agencies responsible for implementing this framework also must vigorously exercise their authority to help ensure the safety and soundness of nonbank firms whose failure could threaten the stability of the financial system. Broad-based application of the principle of consolidated supervision would also serve to eliminate gaps in oversight that would otherwise allow risk-taking to migrate from more-regulated to less-regulated sectors.

Fourth, continued strong and concerted efforts are needed to improve the financial infrastructure—or "plumbing"—that supports the trading, payments, clearing, and settlement activities that are so critical to the functioning of the financial system. I have described elsewhere the various steps that the Federal Reserve is taking in coordination with other supervisors and market participants to improve the resiliency of over-the-counter derivative markets and the market for triparty repurchase agreements. Improvements in these areas should reduce the likelihood that the failure of any individual institution would have substantial spillover effects on other financial institutions or the broader markets, and thereby make it less likely that the government would need to intervene.

Finally, an important element of addressing the too-big-to-fail problem is the development of an improved resolution regime in the United States that permits the orderly resolution of a systemically important nonbank financial firm. We have such a regime for insured depository institutions, but it is clear we need something similar for systemically important nonbank financial entities. Improved resolution procedures for these firms would help reduce the too-big-to-fail problem by giving the government the option of safely winding down a systemically important firm rather than keeping it operating.

Reducing Procyclicality

In the current environment, financial institutions of all sizes are trying to meet the needs of creditworthy borrowers while at the same time maintaining sufficient capital and other resources to weather the ongoing crisis. Capital rules, accounting policies, and other regulatory standards should not make this job even more difficult by encouraging excessively procyclical behavior by financial institutions—that is, behavior that causes financial institutions to tighten credit in downturns and ease credit in booms more than is justified by changes in the creditworthiness of borrowers.

No one questions the underlying objectives of capital rules and accounting standards, which are to ensure the safety and soundness of financial institutions and to accurately and transparently disclose an institution's financial condition, respectively. However, some aspects of existing capital rules and accounting standards may unduly magnify the ups and downs in the financial system and the economy. For example, the capital rules require banks to maintain capital ratios that meet or exceed fixed minimum standards. Because banks typically find raising capital to be difficult in economic downturns or periods of financial stress, their best means of boosting regulatory capital ratios during difficult periods may be to reduce new lending, perhaps more so than is justified by the credit environment. Moreover, as many institutions and auditors will attest, determining the appropriate valuation of illiquid or idiosyncratic assets can be very challenging, especially in highly strained market conditions. The economic downturn also has renewed the debate concerning the appropriate levels of loan loss reserves over the cycle. . . .

A Role for Community Banks

I want to conclude by encouraging you as community bankers to operate prudently in the current environment, but not to let fear drive your decisions. You should all continue to exercise good risk management—including strong underwriting for individual exposures and proper management of credit concentrations in your portfolios. You should also be certain that any deterioration in asset quality and borrowers' conditions are accurately identified, measured, and managed. And you should take steps to maintain a strong financial condition with sufficient capital and liquidity levels as preparation for any future economic and financial uncertainty. By doing so, you can ensure that your institutions can continue to provide a steady and consistent source of credit to businesses and borrowers for years to come. If community banks are prudent but opportunistic in extending credit to strong borrowers, they will help the economy recover while benefiting from that recovery themselves.

"For a free market system to be successful, firms must be allowed to fail . . . [whether it is] a small bank in Tulsa or a large international financial conglomerate in New York City."

Big Banks Should Be Allowed to Fail

Thomas M. Hoenig

Thomas M. Hoenig is the president of the Federal Reserve Bank of Kansas City.

In the following viewpoint, Hoenig takes issue with the belief that the failure of large financial institutions would pose too great a threat to the economy, and suggests a process for dealing with banks that have been called too big to fail. He argues that his process is similar to ones used successfully in Sweden in the 1990s and by the Reconstruction Finance Corporation in the 1930s in the United States to deal with failed banks.

As you read, consider the following questions:

1. What four principles does the author recommend be considered in addressing the financial crisis?

Thomas M. Hoenig, "Too Big to Fail or Too Big to Save? Examining the Systemic Threats of Large Financial Institutions," U.S. Congress, Joint Economic Committee, April 21, 2009.

2. What are the three categories Hoenig recommends for classifying banks based on their solvency?

3. How does the author recommend dealing with a large financial institution that has failed?

As you all know, we are in the middle of a very serious financial crisis, and our economy is under significant stress. There has been much debate about how we should address these challenges, but regardless of the method one supports, all agree that the economy will not recover until the financial system is stabilized and credit flows improve.

The restoration of normal financial market activity depends on how we deal with the problems of our largest financial institutions. It has been a little more than a year since the first major government rescue occurred with Bear Stearns being acquired by JPMorgan. Since then, numerous programs have been enacted and trillions of dollars of public funds have been committed, much of it directly to our largest institutions. Despite these well-intentioned efforts, the problems remain, and the public's dissatisfaction with how their money is being spent grows.

It is not surprising that the initial measures taken in this crisis were ad hoc. The depth and extent of the problems were not anticipated. However, more than a year has passed and the challenge that still remains is to define a plan that addresses the significant asset problems embedded in our largest institutions. We must provide financial firms, investors and consumers with a clear and fair plan for dealing with firms that many call "too big to fail."

Last month [March 2009], I gave a speech that outlined a resolution framework and a plan for how we should deal with these large systemically important financial firms. I believe that failure is an option. Those who disagree with my resolution proposal say that it is unworkable. In my remarks today, I will offer more details about how the process would work and explain why I think it is the best solution for getting our financial system and economy on the road to recovery.

Principles for a Resolution

For a free market system to be successful, firms must be allowed to fail based upon a predefined set of rules and principles that market participants can rely on when determining their strategies and making decisions. This is particularly important for problem financial institutions. These key principles should apply if we are talking about a small bank in Tulsa or a large international financial conglomerate in New York City.

The first principle is to properly understand our goals and correctly identify the problems we are attempting to solve. This may sound obvious. However, when we are in the middle of a crisis where more than a half million people are losing their jobs every month, it is tempting to pour money into the institutions thinking that it will correct the problem and get credit flowing once again. Also, rather than letting the market system objectively discipline the firms through failure and stockholder loss, we tend to micromanage the institutions and punish those within reach.

This lack of confidence in the market's remedy is most acute for our largest financial institutions, which have publically disclosed substantial losses. The question that the supervisory authorities must answer is whether the losses are large enough to threaten the solvency of any of these firms. This assessment is the first step in determining actions necessary to restoring public confidence in our financial system.

A second principle is that we must do what is best for the overall economy and not what is best for one group. We need to make sure that when one financial firm fails, the resolution process does not cause significant disruptions to financial markets and the economy or make the current problems worse. Furthermore, we must do it for the lowest possible cost so that we don't create a long-term fiscal burden on taxpayers.

It is important to recognize that there are not just the direct costs but, more importantly, long-term costs to the economy and financial system. The direct cost of resolving a failed bank, such as the government bearing some of a failed bank's losses, is simple to determine. However, it is much more difficult to know the costs from some of the unintended consequences. For example, market discipline is reduced when a resolution process does not make management, shareholders and creditors bear the costs of their actions.

The third principle is equity of treatment. Regardless of an institution's size, complexity or location, the resolution process must provide consistent treatment of a failing institution's owners, managers, employees and customers. The process must be transparent and clearly stated so that everyone understands what to expect if they gamble with the firm's assets.

When talking about equity of treatment, it is important to recognize that a single process can lead to different outcomes. For example, if any bank is examined and found to be insolvent, it needs to go through the resolution process with the owners losing their investment. However, the eventual outcomes for the institution can be different. A smaller bank's assets and deposits will likely be sold to another bank. In the case of a larger bank, the firm might be temporarily operated as a bridge bank before either being sold or reprivatized. Regardless, it is important that the banks go through the same process or else an incentive will be created for banks to take on excessive risks in an effort to grow large enough to gain favorable treatment.

A final principle is that we must base the resolution process on facts about what works and what does not work. One way to do this is to look at past financial crises. This is not the first financial crisis, and we can learn a lot about what will

What Would George Bailey Do?

I doubt . . . that George Bailey [hero in the film *It's a Wonderful Life*] would support a quasi-public bailout of Bear Stearns or any other threatened financial giant. He would probably agree with many contemporary analysts that Bear Stearns has been an unusually nasty company without a shred of public-spiritedness. In its failure, it would merely have reaped what it had sown. Bailey would dismiss as preposterous claims that the fate of the American and world economics hinged on this rogue company's survival.

Over the long haul, George Bailey would probably try to return the housing and mortgage industries to their real purpose: providing homes to families. He would support limiting the tax deduction on home-mortgage interest to one principal residence per family. He might even favor a cap on the amount that could be deducted, so that only good shelter—not princely luxury—enjoyed favored tax treatment. And he would probably redistribute tax benefits to families according to their number of dependent children, raising either the child tax credit or the per-capita deduction for children—or both.

As his father had noted, "These families have children." That, I believe, would be George Bailey's touchstone for reform.

Allan C. Carlson,
American Conservative, *May 5, 2008.*

and will not be successful by looking back at our own history with financial crises, as well as at the experiences in other countries.

Identifying the Problem

With these principles in mind, how should we go about resolving the current problems at our largest institutions?

First, we must determine both the location and size of the losses. Admittedly, it will not be easy. These firms are very large—the four largest bank holding companies each have more than $1 trillion of assets, which accounts for about half of the banking industry's assets. They have offices around the world, and they are involved in many complex businesses. But in order to repair the financial system, we must get the best estimates of the condition and viability of these firms, and we must require them to reflect their losses in their financial statements. . . .

Once we determine a bank's status, we would classify these institutions into three categories, depending on whether they are solvent and what their prospects are for continuing as an ongoing concern.

The first category would be firms whose operations are strong and whose equity remains above minimum requirements. These firms would not require much government support, if any. Some might need to raise additional capital to provide a greater cushion against the losses they may suffer during the current crisis. But these institutions are basically sound and should be able to raise private capital.

The second category would be those institutions whose equity temporarily falls below minimum requirements but are expected to recover in a reasonable period of time as economic conditions improve. These firms have generally sound management, who may have made some mistakes and suffered greater losses than normal due to the economic downturn. It is reasonable to expect these banks to raise additional private capital. However, the government may need to provide some capital in the form of preferred shares and possibly some warrants in return. As an equity holder, the government would have an oversight role regarding the firms' operations and activities.

The final category is for the institutions that are no longer viable either because of liquidity problems or their equity capital is currently negative or it is likely to become negative, based on reasonable expectations of future market and economic conditions. These firms, which would likely soon become equity insolvent without government protections and guarantees, would be declared insolvent by the regulatory authority. Shareholders would be forced to bear the full cost of the positions they have taken and risk losing their investment. Senior management and the board of directors would be replaced because they are responsible for the failed strategy.

A Resolution Process

The question then becomes how to resolve these failed institutions while minimizing the cost and disruption to the economy.

The method most often used when a bank fails is to arrange for a sale of its assets and an assumption of its liabilities by another institution. For these extremely large firms, there are a couple of significant roadblocks preventing this solution. First, the acquiring firm must have the capacity for the acquisition, which means it would have to be in the same size range as the failed institution. And secondly, if such a deal was forged, it would create an even larger firm with greater systemic risks to the economy.

Instead, an extremely large firm that has failed would have to be temporarily operated as a conservatorship or a bridge organization and then reprivatized as quickly as is economically feasible. We cannot simply add more capital without a change in the firm's ownership and management and expect different outcomes in the future.

Experience shows that this approach has worked. The best example was with the failure of Continental Illinois National Bank and its holding company in 1984. . . .

A Record of Success

It is understandable that there are concerns about letting these large firms fail, but it should be noted that the program I have just described has a record of success elsewhere.

The economic situation in Sweden in the early 1990s was similar to that in the United States today. Its financial system was dominated by six large banks that accounted for 90 percent of the industry's assets. Sweden took decisive steps to identify losses in its major financial institutions. The viable Swedish banks were soon recapitalized, largely through private sources, and public authorities quickly took over two large insolvent banks and spun off their bad assets to be managed within a separate entity. Sweden was able to systematically restore confidence in its financial system, and although it took several years to work down and sell off all of the bad assets, there was minimal net cost to the taxpayers.

Some argue that the Swedish situation is not a valid comparison because it dealt with only six banks. In addition, some argue that the Swedish system was much less complex, and that the Swedish government had to work out primarily commercial real estate loans instead of the complex financial assets, structured securities and derivatives that we would have to work out today.

These are valid concerns, but I would point out, first, that although the United States has several thousand banks, only 19 have more than $100 billion of assets, and that after supervisory authorities evaluate their condition, it is likely that few would require further government intervention. Second, as for complexity, I would point out that real estate assets involve considerable complexity, no less so than many financial derivatives.

Another important example is the Reconstruction Finance Corporation (RFC), which was used to deal with banking problems in the United States in the 1930s. The RFC followed a process very similar to what I have described. It began by examining problem banks and writing down the bad assets to realistic economic values, making any needed and appropriate changes in bank management, injecting public equity as needed into these banks, and returning the banks to private ownership. The RFC proved to be highly successful in recapitalizing banks, and like Sweden, there was essentially no net cost to taxpayers. . . .

Let me make two final points.

First, the debate over the resolution of the largest financial firms is often sensationalized because it is framed in terms of nationalizing failed institutions. It is also pointed out that government officials may not be effective managers of private business concerns.

In response, I would note that no firm would be nationalized in this program. Nationalization is the process of the government taking over a going concern with the intent of operating it. Though a bridge institution is the most likely outcome when a large financial firm fails, the goal is for the firm to be reprivatized as quickly as possible. In addition, subject to regulatory agency oversight, the bridge firm would be managed by private sector managers selected for their experience in operating well-run, large, complex organizations.

The second point is related to the complexity issue, which is that it would be hard to find enough people with the required knowledge, experience and skills to fill the open positions. Going back to the Continental Illinois example, we were able to do it then. More generally: The United States is a vast country with a tremendous amount of management resources in a broad-based economic and industrial system. If the United States does not have the talent to run these firms, then we are much worse off than I thought. I refuse to accept that conclusion.

Periodical Bibliography

The following articles have been selected to supplement the diverse views presented in this chapter.

Andrew Clark	"U.S. Banking Crisis Far from Over, Congress Warns," *Guardian* (Manchester, UK), August 11, 2009.
Thomas F. Cooley	"A Captive FDIC," *Forbes*, April 15, 2009.
Rob Cox and Hugo Dixon	"Reconsidering Deposit Insurance," *New York Times*, October 1, 2008.
Eric Dash	"If It's Too Big to Fail, Is It Too Big to Exist?" *New York Times*, June 20, 2009.
James Doran	"It's Groundhog Day for Obama's Economic Team," *Spectator*, May 23, 2009.
Douglas J. Elliott	"Bank Stress Test Results," *Huffington Post*, May 12, 2009.
David Ellis	"The Messy Issue of 'Too Big to Fail,'" *CNNMoney*, July 31, 2009.
Joan Goldwasser, Kimberly Lankford, and Pat Mertz Esswein	"Is My Money *Still* Safe?" *Kiplinger's Personal Finance*, October 2008.
Paul Krugman	"The Market Mystique," *New York Times*, March 27, 2009.
Seeking Alpha	"'Too Big to Fail' Cause of Current Community Bank Failures," August 2, 2009.
Shawn Tully	"Will the Banks Survive?" *Fortune*, February 27, 2009.
24/7 Wall St.	"More Quickly than It Began, the Financial Crisis Is Over," *Time*, April 10, 2009.
Peter J. Wallison	"Too Big to Fail, or Succeed," *Wall Street Journal*, June 19, 2009.

CHAPTER 3

How Should the U.S. Banking System Be Fixed?

Chapter Preface

Speaking to an assembly of Wall Street bankers on September 14, 2009, on the one-year anniversary of the collapse of Lehman Brothers that catapulted global markets into a financial crisis, President Barack Obama laid out his plan for reforming the U.S. banking system.

"We are calling on the financial industry to join us in a constructive effort to update the rules and regulatory structure to meet the challenges of this new century. That is what my administration seeks to do. . . .

"Taken together, we are proposing the most ambitious overhaul of the financial system since the Great Depression. But I want to emphasize that these reforms are rooted in a simple principle: We ought to set clear rules of the road that promote transparency and accountability. That's how we'll make certain that markets foster responsibility, not recklessness, and reward those who compete honestly and vigorously within the system, instead of those who try to game the system."

It was a message that most in his audience received politely but lukewarmly. A position popular in the banking community was articulated by Jeffrey Lacker, chief of the Richmond (Virginia) Federal Reserve, who argued that action by private enterprise, not government policy, is the prudent course.

"The leading proposals before Congress concentrate almost exclusively on expanding government protection and regulation, but I believe we would be better off placing greater reliance on market-based incentives for prudent risk-management," Lacker said in a speech the same day as the president's address.

However, several commentators argued that the Obama administration's proposals do not go far enough. The next day, Nobel Prize–winning economist Joseph Stiglitz posted an article critical of the talk on the British newspaper the *Guardian*'s Web site, stating:

> Last night Barack Obama defended his administration's response to the financial crisis, but the reality is that a year on from Lehmans's collapse, it has failed to take adequate steps to restrict institutions' size, their risk-taking, and their interconnectedness. Indeed, it has allowed the big banks to become even bigger—just as it has failed to stem the flow of profligate executive bonuses. Obama's call on Wall Street yesterday to support "the most ambitious overhaul of the financial system since the Great Depression" is welcome—but the devil, as ever, will be in the details.

These divergent statements are emblematic of the lack of consensus surrounding the difficult issue of reforming the U.S. banking system. In the following chapter, politicians, commentators, and economists offer a variety of proposals for mending the system.

| *"A government takeover of our banking system . . . is the only solution."*

Banks Should Be Nationalized

Joseph E. Stiglitz

Joseph E. Stiglitz is a professor of economics at Columbia University. He received the Nobel Prize in Economics in 2001.

In the following viewpoint, Stiglitz calls for the temporary nationalization of inadequately capitalized banks. He argues that many banks are in effect bankrupt, their true conditions hidden by their shady accounting practices. Stiglitz supports the concept of creating Good Banks and Bad Banks to dispose of toxic assets in an orderly fashion during the process of nationalization. He also holds out hope that restructured banks could be sold at a profit, thus recouping some of the bailout funding.

As you read, consider the following questions:

1. What are the roles of the Good Bank and the Bad Bank in the solution to the banking crisis that Stiglitz supports?

Joseph E. Stiglitz, "A Bank Bailout That Works," *The Nation*, March 23, 2009, pp. 22, 24, 26–27. Copyright © 2009 by The Nation Magazine/The Nation Company, Inc. Reproduced by permission.

2. What are the reasons the author gives for his disagreement with the argument that the government cannot be trusted to run a bank?

3. Why does Stiglitz believe that employees in a government-run bank will behave better than in one run by private enterprise?

The news that even [former Federal Reserve Board chairman] Alan Greenspan and Senator Chris Dodd are supporting bank nationalization shows how desperate the situation has become. It has been obvious for some time that a government takeover of our banking system—perhaps along the lines of what Norway and Sweden did in the '90s—is the only solution. It should be done, and done quickly, before even more bailout money is wasted.

The problem with America's banks is not just one of liquidity.[1] Years of reckless behavior, including bad lending and gambling with derivatives, have left them, in effect, bankrupt. If our government were playing by the rules—which require shutting down banks with inadequate capital—many, if not most, banks would go out of business. But because faulty accounting practices don't force banks to mark down all their assets to current market prices, they may nominally meet capital requirements—at least for a while. . . .

The Good Bank Proposal

Gradually America is realizing that we must do something—now. We already have a framework for dealing with banks whose capital is inadequate. We should use it, and quickly, with perhaps some modifications to take care of the unusual nature of today's problems. There are several ways we can proceed. One innovative proposal (variants of which have been floated by Willem Buiter at the London School of Eco-

1. Liquidity is the ability of an asset to be quickly converted to cash without affecting the asset's price.

nomics and by [financier and philanthropist] George Soros) entails the creation of a Good Bank. Rather than dump the bad assets on the government, we would strip out the good assets—those that can be easily priced. If the value of claims by depositors and other claims that we decide need to be protected is less than the value of the assets, then the government would write a check to the Old Bank (we could call it the Bad Bank). If the reverse is true, then the government would have a senior claim on the Old Bank. In normal times, it would be easy to recapitalize the Good Bank privately. These are not normal times, so the government might have to run the bank for a while.

Meanwhile, the Old Bank would be left with the task of disposing of its toxic assets[2] as best it can. Because the Old Bank's capital is inadequate, it couldn't take deposits, unless it found enough capital privately to recapitalize itself. How much shareholders and bondholders got would depend on how well management did in disposing of these assets—and how well they did in ensuring that management didn't overpay itself.

The Good Bank proposal has the advantage of avoiding the N-word: nationalization.[3] Some believe a more polite term, "conservatorship" as it was called in the case of Fannie Mae, may be more palatable. It should be clear, though, that whatever it is called, the Good Bank proposal entails little more than playing by longstanding rules, a variant of standard practices to deal with firms whose liabilities exceed their assets.

The Private Sector Failed

Those who say the government cannot be trusted to allocate capital efficiently sound unconvincing these days. After all, it's not as though the private sector did a very good job. No

2. Toxic assets are those assets whose value has dropped so sharply that they are no longer saleable.
3. Nationalization is taking an enterprise into public ownership by a national government.

The Case for Nationalization

The case for nationalization rests on three observations.

First, some major banks are dangerously close to the edge. . . .

Second, banks must be rescued. The collapse of Lehman Brothers almost destroyed the world financial system, and we can't risk letting much bigger institutions like Citigroup or Bank of America implode.

Third, while banks must be rescued, the U.S. government can't afford, fiscally or politically, to bestow huge gifts on bank shareholders.

Paul Krugman, New York Times, *February 23, 2009.*

peacetime government has wasted resources on the scale of America's private financial system. Wall Street's incentives structures were designed to encourage shortsighted and excessively risky behavior. The bankers were supposed to understand risk, but they did not understand the most elementary principles of information asymmetry, risk correlation and fat-tailed distributions. Most of them, while they may have been ethically challenged, were really guided in their behavior by the perverse incentives they championed. The result was that they did not even serve their shareholders well; from 2004 to 2008, net profits of many of the major banks were negative.

There is every reason to believe that a temporarily nationalized bank will behave much better—even if most of the employees are still the same—simply because we will have changed the perverse incentives. Besides, a government-run bank might spend some time and money teaching its employees about risk management, good lending practices, social responsibility and ethics. The experience elsewhere, including in the Scandinavian countries, shows that the whole process can be done well—and when the economy is eventually restored to prosperity, the profitable banks can be returned to the private sector. What is required is not rocket science. Banks simply need to get back to what they were supposed to do: lending money, on a prudent basis, to businesses and households, based not just on collateral but on a good assessment of the use to which borrowers will put the money and their ability to repay it.

A Plan for Bad Assets

Meanwhile, there needs to be an orderly plan for disposing of the old bad assets. There is no magic in moving them around from one owner to another. In some countries, government agencies (often hiring private subcontractors) have done a good job of selling off the assets. Other countries (including some hit in the East Asia crisis a decade ago) have had an unfortunate experience, bringing in investment banks and hedge funds[4] to dispose of their assets. These institutions simply held them for the short time it took the economy to recover and made a huge capital gain at the expense of the country's taxpayers. To add insult to injury, some even took advantage of tax havens to avoid paying taxes on those huge profits. These experiences suggest caution in turning to hedge funds and other investment firms.

Every downturn comes to an end. Eventually we will be able to sell the restructured banks at a good price—though, one hopes, not one based on the irrational exuberant expectation of another financial bubble. The notion that we will make a profit from the bailouts—which the financial sector tried to convince us were "investments"—seems to have dropped from public discourse. But at least we can use the

4. Hedge funds are pooled private investment funds that seek to maximize returns with strategies that include unconventional investments and investments that cannot easily be converted to cash, such as real estate.

147

proceeds of the eventual sale of the restructured banks to pay down the huge deficit that this financial debacle will have brought onto our nation.

"*The Obama administration should declare that nationalization of any major bank is off the table.*"

Nationalizing Banks Will Not Work

William M. Isaac

William M. Isaac is chairman of The Secura Group, a financial services consulting firm. He was chairman of the Federal Deposit Insurance Corporation (FDIC) from 1981–1985.

During Isaac's tenure as FDIC chairman, Continental Illinois Bank, the country's seventh largest bank, was nationalized and taken over by the FDIC. Although he admits that nationalization worked successfully at Continental, in the following viewpoint Isaac contends that there are significant differences between its circumstances and the circumstances surrounding big banks in 2008–2009, and that these differences make bank nationalization not a viable option.

As you read, consider the following questions:

1. What is the difference in scale between Continental Illinois Bank and the ten largest banking companies in 2009, as described by Isaac?

2. What does the author see as the three main differences between Continental and the ten largest banking companies in 2009?

3. Why does Isaac feel that Swedish bank nationalization is not relevant to the U.S. banking situation?

People who should know better have been speculating publicly that the government might need to nationalize our largest banks. This irresponsible chatter is causing tremendous turmoil in financial markets. The Obama administration needs to make clear immediately that nationalization—government seizing control of ownership and operations of a company—is not a viable option.

Speaking from Experience

Unlike the talking heads, I have actually nationalized a large bank. When I headed the Federal Deposit Insurance Corporation (FDIC) during the banking crisis of the 1980s, the FDIC recapitalized and took control of Continental Illinois Bank, which was then the country's seventh largest bank.

The FDIC purchased Continental's problem loans at a big discount and hired the bank to manage and collect the loans under an incentive arrangement. We received 80% ownership of the company, which increased to 100% based on the losses suffered by the FDIC on the bad loans.

We replaced Continental's senior management and most of its board of directors. We required the bank to submit a business plan to shrink to half its size within three years. All major decisions required FDIC approval, including the hiring, firing and compensation of senior management, and the undertaking of new business endeavors.

The takeover occurred in 1984, the FDIC completed the sale of its ownership stake seven years later, and Continental was purchased by Bank of America in 1994. The old shareholders ultimately received nothing, all creditors and preferred

A Misguided Premise

The [claim that the] only way to fix the banks is to nationalize them . . . is a misguided premise. The announcement of nationalization would undermine confidence in the financial system and send shudders through the investment community. Politicizing lending decisions and the credit allocation process would be destructive for the economy. Nationalization also would give the false impression that all banks are insolvent.

Kenneth D. Lewis, Wall Street Journal, *March 9, 2009.*

shareholders came out whole, and the FDIC suffered what we considered a reasonable loss: $1.6 billion.

So, you might wonder, what's so bad about nationalization? It appears to have worked well at Continental.

Continental's Case Was Simpler

Let's begin with the fact that today our 10 largest banking companies hold some two-thirds of the nation's banking assets, and some are enormously complex. Continental had less than 2% of the nation's banking assets, and by today's standards it was a plain-vanilla bank. This is important for three reasons.

First, any bank we nationalize will be forced, both by the regulators and the marketplace, to shrink dramatically. We are in the middle of a serious economic downturn where deflation is a realistic concern. Do we really think that dismantling our largest banks would be helpful? I don't.

What's more, we won't be able to stop at nationalizing one or two banks. If we start down that path, the short sellers and other speculators that the Securities and Exchange Commission still refuses to re-regulate will target for destruction one after another of our largest banks.

Second, for nationalization to work there needs to be a reasonable exit strategy. In the case of Continental, we had scores of options for returning the bank to private hands, including a public offering or a sale to any number of domestic and foreign banks and investor groups.

Today, who has the wherewithal, legal authority, and desire to purchase our largest banks? No one comes to mind, particularly if we rule out foreign groups, which I suspect would not pass muster due to national security concerns about ceding that much power over our economy to foreign powers.

Third, who will run these companies when we dismiss the existing senior managers and board members? We had significant difficulties attracting quality people to Continental even without today's limits on compensation.

So-called experts frequently cite the success of the Swedish experience with bank nationalization in the last decade. Nothing could be less relevant. Sweden's population, economy and banking system are roughly the size of Ohio's. Sweden's largest bank is roughly 10% the size of each of our three largest banking companies. Moreover, Sweden nationalized only Gota Bank—and that was after it had already collapsed.

The Obama administration should declare that nationalization of any major bank is off the table; that the government stands behind our entire banking system; and that our banks will continue to receive a nonvoting form of equity capital, such as convertible preferred stock, from the government to the extent needed. Yesterday's [February 23, 2009,] joint announcement to this effect by the Federal Reserve, FDIC, the Comptroller of the Currency, and the Treasury is a critical step toward healing our banking system and economy. Well done.

*"I want ... clear lines of authority and
strong checks and balances that build
... confidence in our financial system."*

More Regulation of Banking Is Needed

Christopher J. Dodd

*Christopher J. Dodd, a Democrat, is the senior senator from the
state of Connecticut and the chair of the Senate Banking, Housing, and Urban Affairs Committee. He also briefly ran for president in the 2008 campaign.*

*In the following viewpoint, which comes from Dodd's open-
ing statement during a hearing on modernizing bank supervision and regulation before the U.S. Senate Committee on Banking, Housing, and Urban Affairs, he makes the case for the need
for broad and comprehensive reform of the financial regulatory
system. He suggests that given the level of expertise that this
oversight will entail, that it might properly reside within the
Federal Deposit Insurance Corporation.*

As you read, consider the following questions:

1. According to the author, what is the primary focus of
   the Federal Reserve?

Christopher J. Dodd, "Modernizing Bank Supervision and Regulation," opening statement of Christopher J. Dodd, chairman, U.S. Senate Committee on Banking, Housing,
and Urban Affairs, March 19, 2009.

2. What are some of the failures of the Federal Reserve that Dodd cites?

3. The author gives some reasons supporting the creation of a consolidated entity to oversee systemic risk to the financial community. What rationale does he give to support this suggestion?

A year ago [2008], this Committee [Senate Banking, Housing, and Urban Affairs] heard from witnesses on two separate occasions that the banking system was sound and that the vast majority of banks would be well positioned to weather the storm.

A year later and taxpayers are forced to pump billions of dollars into our major banking institutions to keep them afloat. Meanwhile, every day, 20,000 people lose their jobs, 10,000 families lose their homes and credit, the lifeblood of our economy, is frozen solid.

Get Banking Reform Right

People are furious right now, as they should be. But history will judge whether we make the right decisions. And as President [Barack] Obama told the Congress last month [February 2009], we cannot afford to govern out of anger or yield to the politics of the moment as we prepare to make choices that will shape the future of our country literally for decades to come.

We need to get this right.

We must learn from mistakes and draw upon those lessons to shape a new framework for financial services regulation—an integrated, transparent and comprehensive architecture that serves the American people well through the 21st century.

Instead of the race to the bottom we saw in the run-up to this crisis, I want a race to the top—with clear lines of authority and strong checks and balances that build the confidence in our financial system that is so essential to our economic growth and stability.

Certainly, there is a case to be made for a so-called "systemic risk regulator" within that framework.

Whether or not those vast powers will reside at the Fed [Federal Reserve] remains an open question. The Fed's primary focus is on the conduct of monetary policy and its ever-ballooning portfolio and its expanding balance sheet which could reach $3 trillion. And that is to say nothing of its increasing number of responsibilities, and the obvious mistakes the Fed made in the run-up to the current crisis.

Regulating Risk with FDIC

As [Federal Reserve] Chairman [Ben] Bernanke very recently said, the role of systemic risk regulation will entail a great deal of expertise, analytical sophistication, and the capacity to process large amounts of disparate information.

I agree with Chairman Bernanke, which is why I wonder whether it wouldn't make more sense to give the authority to resolve failing systemically-important institutions to the agency with actual expertise in that area: the FDIC [Federal Deposit Insurance Corporation].

If the events of this week [March 19, 2009,] have taught us anything, it is that the unwinding of these institutions can sap both public dollars and public confidence essential to getting our economy back on track. This underscores the importance of establishing a mechanism to resolve these failing institutions.

From its failure to protect consumers, to regulate mortgage lending, to effectively oversee bank holding companies, the instances in which the Fed has failed to execute its existing authority are numerous.

In a crisis that has taught the American people many hard-earned lessons, perhaps the most important is that no institu-

An Approach to Regulation

There should be three major objectives of regulation, as follows.

- To make sure that there is micro-prudential supervisions, so that customers and taxpayers are protected against excessive risk taking that may cause a single institution to fail.

- To make sure that whole financial sector retains its balance and does not become unstable. That means someone has to warn about the build up of risk across several institutions and perhaps take regulatory actions to restrain lending used to purchase assets whose prices are creating a speculative bubble.

- To regulate the conduct of business. That means to watch out for the interests of consumers and investors, whether they are small shareholders in public companies or households deciding whether to take out a mortgage or use a credit card.

In applying this approach, it is vital for both the economy and the financial sector that the Federal Reserve has independence as it makes monetary policy. Experience in the US and around the world supports the view that an independent central bank results in better macro-economic performance and restrains inflationary expectations. An independent Fed setting monetary policy is essential.

Martin Neil Baily, Testimony to Senate Committee on Banking, Housing, and Urban Affairs, August 4, 2009.

tion should ever be "too big to fail." And going forward, we should consider how that lesson applies not only to our financial institutions—but also to the government entities charged with regulating them.

Replacing Citibank-sized financial institutions with Citibank-sized regulators would be a grave mistake.

This crisis has illustrated all too well the dangers posed to the consumer and our economy when we consolidate too much power in too few hands with far too little transparency and accountability.

Further, as former Fed Chairman [Paul] Volcker has suggested, there may well be an inherent conflict of interest between prudential supervision—that is, the day-to-day regulation of our banks—and monetary policy—the Fed's primary mission and an essential one.

One idea that has been suggested that could complement and support an entity that oversees systemic risk is a consolidated safety and soundness regulator.

The regulatory arbitrage[1], duplication and inefficiency that comes with having multiple federal banking regulators was at least as much of a problem in creating this crisis as the Fed's inability to see this crisis coming and its failure to protect consumers and investors.

And so, systemic risk is important—but no more so than the risk to consumers and depositors, the engine behind our banking system. Creating that race to the top starts with building from the bottom up.

That is why I am equally interested in what we do at the prudential supervision level to empower regulators—the first line of defense for consumers and depositors—and increase the transparency that is absolutely essential to checks and balances and a healthy financial system.

1. Arbitrage is a strategy in which investors profit from temporary discrepancies between the prices of the stocks comprising an index, or list of stocks, and the price of a futures contract on that index. By buying either the stocks or the futures contract and selling the other, an investor can sometimes exploit market inefficiency for a profit.

Each of these issues leads us to a simple conclusion: the need for broad, comprehensive reform is clear. We cannot afford to address the future of our financial system piecemeal or ad hoc, without considering the role every actor at every level must play in creating a stable banking system that helps our economy grow for decades to come.

> "Congress can create a better regulatory
> structure and can expand regulatory
> powers, but in the end, the one thing it
> can't legislate is the good judgment of
> the regulators."

Reinventing Regulation

Steven Pearlstein

Steven Pearlstein is a columnist for the Washington Post *who won the Pulitzer Prize for Commentary in 2008.*

In the following viewpoint, Pearlstein recommends consolidating the regulation of all financial institutions into one entity—the Federal Deposit Insurance Corporation. He also believes that there is a role for the Federal Reserve in preventing a systemic breakdown of financial markets. He warns, however, that the current crisis would not have occurred if the existing regulators had been doing their jobs.

As you read, consider the following questions:

1. What are the reasons the author gives for recommending the FDIC as the consolidated regulator of the financial industry?

2. What are the reasons Pearlstein gives for rejecting the role of the Federal Reserve as systemic regulator?

3. What is the problem the author cites with treating too-big-to-fail banks differently?

During President [Barack] Obama's speech yesterday [April 14, 2009,] on the economy at Georgetown University, it was hard to miss that the biggest applause lines were those that criticized Wall Street for reckless risk-taking and squandering so much wealth and talent. To make sure it never happens again, the president challenged Congress to come up with an entirely new regulatory regime by the end of the year.

Good luck with that.

To begin with, what's the rush? Most of the damage has already been done, and at this point the industry is still in the midst of a massive restructuring. Until that process has finished and it is clear what entities, what products and what markets emerge from this restructuring, trying to figure out how to regulate them would seem a bit premature.

I also can't think of another sector that has proven itself so adept over the years at blocking even minor reforms, let alone something as ambitious as what the president has in mind. With so many conflicting interests among well-heeled firms and so many agencies fighting to protect their bureaucratic turf, the most likely outcome is political stalemate. Watching the Senate Banking Committee deal with financial regulation is a bit like watching a cow chew its cud.

Three Roles for Regulators

That said, it is probably useful to begin thinking about what the new architecture for financial regulation should look like.

Step one is to consolidate day-to-day "safety and soundness" regulation of all financial firms—banks, investment banks, bank holding companies, insurance companies, hedge funds, housing finance agencies—in a single entity. In the

Better, Not More, Regulation

The past few decades have witnessed a significant expansion in the number of financial regulators and regulations, contrary to the widely held belief that our financial market regulations were "rolled back." While many regulators may have been short-sighted and over-confident in their own ability to spare our financial markets from collapse, this failing is one of regulation, not deregulation. When one scratches below the surface of the "deregulation" argument, it becomes apparent that the usual suspects, like the Gramm-Leach-Bliley Act, did not cause the current crisis and that the supposed refusal of regulators to deal with derivatives and "predatory" mortgages would have had little impact on the actual course of events, as these issues were not central to the crisis. To explain the financial crisis, and avoid the next one, we should look at the failure of regulation, not at mythical deregulation.

Mark A. Calabria, Cato Policy Report, *July/August 2009.*

past, each type of institution was regulated by a different agency. But over time, firms became adept at getting around regulation by finding the cracks between the agencies and playing one regulator off another.

But which of the existing bank regulators should get the assignment as prudential regulator? My vote is to build it around the Federal Deposit Insurance Corp [FDIC]. As an independent agency, the FDIC is a bit more insulated from the political influence wielded by banks and Wall Street firms. The FDIC's insurance culture has fostered a more cautious and conservative regulatory stance and led to a more arm's-length relationship with the banks that favors public disclosure of shortcomings rather than covering them up. As the agency responsible for taking over banks once they fail, the FDIC also has a special insight into costs of regulatory failure.

In addition to the prudential regulator, there will be a need for a separate agency to protect investors and supervise the markets in which stocks, bonds and futures are traded. There is absolutely no credible rationale for dividing the investor-protection responsibility, as we do now, between the Securities and Exchange Commission [SEC] and the Commodity Futures Trading Commission. Nor, as we've learned from the [insurance giant] AIG debacle, is there any reason to continue to exempt credit-default swaps[1] and other derivative[2] instruments from all regulation? Only the stubborn determination of members of the House and Senate agriculture committees to protect political contributions from the futures[3] and derivatives industry stands in the way of consolidating all of these functions at the more aggressive SEC.

The recent troubles also suggest the need for yet a third regulator, whose sole mission is to prevent breakdowns of the entire financial system. This uber-regulator [super-regulator] would have broad powers to gather whatever information it needs—from other regulators or directly from any financial institution. It would need the power to order those other regulators to take steps to reduce those risks. And if all else fails, it would need the ability to provide liquidity to financial markets and take over major financial institutions that are about to fail. This sounds like a natural role for the Federal Reserve.

1. A credit default swap (CDS) is a transaction where the buyer of a bond or loan makes payments to the seller, who guarantees the creditworthiness of the product. The buyer receives a payment from the seller if the product goes into default.
2. A derivative is a financial instrument whose value is derived from an underlying asset, index, event, value, or condition. The derivative itself is merely a contract to exchange cash or assets over time based on fluctuations in the underlying assets. Most derivatives are characterized by high leverage, or debt.
3. In the futures industry, investors contract to buy or sell a specified commodity of standardized quality at a certain date in the future, at a market-determined price. The contracts are traded on a futures exchange.

Regulation by Fed a Bad Idea

As part of the Fed's [Federal Reserve] role as systemic regulator, Treasury Secretary Tim Geithner has proposed that the central bank also serve as the day-to-day regulator of any financial institution over a certain size. That's a terrible idea.

For starters, the Fed has proven itself a soft touch when it comes to day-to-day bank supervision. For nearly two decades under Chairman Alan Greenspan, the Fed saw its role as encouraging financial innovation through deregulation, preferring to leave it to markets to discipline the banks. That philosophy is now hardwired into the Fed's culture.

Even worse is Geithner's notion of designating certain banks as too big to fail and then subjecting them to more stringent capital requirements and a special tax that would be used to pay for the occasional government bailout. In practice, that approach is likely to create a competitive imbalance between the biggest banks and everyone else, while inviting the giants to find clever ways to take on extra risk, knowing that the government will always be there to bail them out. Creating two classes of institutions with different rules and different regulators would also invite the kind of regulatory arbitrage and games-playing at which Wall Street excels.

Getting all this right would be useful in preventing future financial crises, but don't confuse it with a panacea [cure-all]. Much of the current crisis could have been prevented if the existing patchwork of agencies, using their existing powers, had simply done their jobs. Congress can create a better regulatory structure and can expand regulatory powers, but in the end, the one thing it can't legislate is the good judgment of the regulators.

> *"Behemoth nationwide banks like Citigroup Inc. and Bank of America Corp. expanded willy-nilly and threw the global economy into recession with their reckless trading."*

If Banks Are Too Big to Fail, Take an Ax to Them

David Pauly

David Pauly is a columnist for Bloomberg News.

In the following viewpoint, Pauly maintains it was the risky actions of big banks that caused the economic crisis. To prevent such a crisis from recurring, he argues that big banks should be broken into pieces. Instead of creating thousands of community banks, Pauly recommends the creation of competing regional banks.

As you read, consider the following questions:

1. What first step does the author recommend before breaking up big banks?

2. Why does the author believe it would be easier to break up investment banks than commercial banks?

3. What problem does the author cite in breaking up big investment and commercial banks?

Every town's Main Street Trust & Savings Bank should be the model for preventing future financial debacles.

Behemoth nationwide banks like Citigroup Inc. and Bank of America Corp. expanded willy-nilly and threw the global economy into recession with their reckless trading.

Breaking them up into smaller pieces would mean that the demise of one wouldn't threaten to bring down the rest. No more trillion-dollar banking system rescues.

Sheila Bair, chairman of the Federal Deposit Insurance Corp., endorsed the notion of limiting bank size Monday when she said the government should abolish its "too big to fail" policy and establish a new authority for taking over and winding down broken financial companies.

Unraveling decades of bank takeovers will have to wait until the current credit crisis ends. The first order is to shore up the banks' capital and get them lending again. That accomplished, the government—whose ownership stake in the banks seems certain to grow in the weeks ahead—can pursue the disassembly.

A good start would be the resurrection of the Glass-Steagall Act, forbidding marriages of commercial banks and investment banks. Main Street Trust & Savings invests in mortgages with sensible down payments, not credit default swaps.

The Obama administration could sell banks in pieces or sell them whole with the stipulation that the buyers divide them up, Simon Johnson, former chief economist for the International Monetary Fund, wrote in the May issue of *The Atlantic* magazine.

Regional Rivals

No one really expects the giants to be broken into thousands of local banks where the chief executive officer knows all the customers. Competing regional banks would be the ticket.

The U.S. could use its antitrust laws to dictate the right size for banks, said Johnson, now a professor at Massachusetts Institute of Technology's Sloan School of Management in Cambridge, Massachusetts. I couldn't reach Johnson to see if he would elaborate on his ideas.

Establishing the criteria through the courts or otherwise might be tricky. Do you lower the limit on the percentage of total deposits a bank can have in the region where it does business? Do you limit a bank's total liabilities?

A breakup might lead to higher costs at the smaller commercial banks. Eliminating redundant expenses is always an excuse for a takeover. The truth was, the banks had to keep making acquisitions and cutting costs in recent years to keep profits growing. While big banks may have been cost-efficient, their subprime mortgage[1] woes betray a deficiency in common sense.

1. Subprime mortgages are those to individuals with poor credit histories who would not be able to qualify for conventional mortgages. Higher interest rates are charged on subprime mortgages than conventional mortgages because of the increased risk of default for lenders.

Conflicts Galore

Breaking up investment banks might be easier since there are inherent conflicts when stock retailing, equity underwritings and merger advice are all under one roof. A new Glass-Steagall would force Bank of America to jettison the newly purchased Merrill Lynch & Co.

Bank of America CEO Kenneth Lewis might not be opposed. Not many months ago, Lewis denigrated the investment banking business. More recently he said the government forced him to go through with the Merrill deal when he wanted to back out because of the Wall Street firm's worsening condition.

Smaller financial institutions might also bring about a welcome reduction in the blather about executive pay. The CEO of the Red River Valley Regional Bank won't dare ask for Citigroup-sized remuneration.

There is a problem in cutting commercial and investment banks down to size: making sure that they still aren't big enough that their failure would bring down others.

The FDIC's Bair suggested in her speech in New York two days ago that size may not be an issue. She said the government can take over and divide a company's assets into "good" and "bad"—forcing stockholders and unsecured creditors to shoulder the cost of the bad.

It may not be that easy. But the sooner the process begins, the better.

> *"The importance placed on the issue of size is deceptive: The problems that caused the 2008 crash also had to do with leverage, liquidity, and the complex connections between banks."*

Big Banks Should Not Be Broken Up

Tim Fernholz

Tim Fernholz is a writing fellow at the American Prospect, *and has had his work printed in publications such as the* Nation *and the* Guardian.

In the following article, Fernholz disagrees with the belief that big banks should be broken up. He explains that size was not the main cause of the 2008 crash and breaking up large banks would prove more difficult than many progressive economists think. Fernholz holds that we need a reform in which a rulebook strikes a compromise between using federal money to keep bad banks alive and simply letting banks fail which, under the current system, would cause a market meltdown.

Tim Fernholz, "The Myth of Too Big to Fail: When It Comes to Banking, Size Isn't the Only Thing That Matters," *The American Prospect*, November 2009. Copyright © 2009 The American Prospect, Inc. All rights reserved. Reproduced with permission from The American Prospect, 11 Beacon Street, Suite 1120, Boston, MA 02108.

As you read, consider the following questions:

1. In the article, what does former Securities and Exchange Commission chair Arthur Levitt claim was the problem with the banks?

2. What is a danger the author sees with the Obama administration's plan?

3. What were some of the restrictions that progressives wanted to have on the initial bailouts?

A mid last fall's financial chaos, executives from Wachovia, at the time the fourth-largest commercial bank in the country, had bad news for their regulators: They were broke. Federal officials deliberated and decided Wachovia was so important to the economy that the government had to save it.

It was only the latest in a series of financial institutions that regulators had deemed "too big to fail." In the preceding months, the government had bailed out Fannie Mac, Freddie Mac, and Bear Stearns, and Congress had passed the controversial $700 billion bill to fund yet more financial-sector rescues. Some of the institutions, like the insurance company American International Group (AIG), weren't even banks.

When the news of Wachovia's failure first reached Federal Deposit Insurance Corporation (FDIC) Chair Sheila Bair, she wanted to liquidate the bank and cut into the pocketbooks of its investors—as she had done with Washington Mutual, the largest U.S. bank failure ever, a few days prior. But Tim Geithner, then president of the New York Federal Reserve Bank, argued strenuously for Bait to invoke her agency's "too big to fail" exception and spend more money to cover the costs of the bank's sale. He worried another collapsing bank would only intensify the financial panic at a time when the government's hands were tied. (While the FDIC can liquidate a commercial bank like Wachovia, the Fed doesn't have the tools to shut down financial institutions, only the ability to prop them up with loans.)

Geithner, now the Treasury secretary, made the right decision at the time, but it was a terrible precedent to set. Sending the message that the government won't let large banks fail in a crisis gives them an unfair advantage over their smaller competitors. Worse, if bankers are rewarded for success and insulated from failure, there is little incentive for prudence and smart management—the problem of moral hazard.

Of all the Orwellian phrases to arise from our financial crisis—"troubled assets," "stress tests," "capital infusion"—"too big to fail" is perhaps the most hated and least understood. Many populists and progressive economists have called on the Obama administration to bust up the banks and make them smaller. "Just break them up," economist Dean Baker argues. "We don't have to turn Citigroup and Bank of America into hundreds of small community banks, just large regional banks that can be safely put through a bankruptcy."

The administration hasn't pursued that course of action, in part because of the political power of the banks and in part because breaking them up isn't as easy as it sounds—it is hard to know what the right size for a bank is, especially in an increasingly global financial market. Further, the importance placed on the issue of size is deceptive: The problems that caused the 2008 crash also had to do with leverage, liquidity, and the complex connections between banks. The banks tied themselves into knots neither they nor their regulators could untie.

"The problem we have had isn't that institutions were too big—it was that there was no uniform way to let them fail without causing an absolute market meltdown," Arthur Levitt, the widely respected former Securities and Exchange Commission chair, told the House Financial Services Committee in September.

If we want to clean up the financial mess, we have to realize that the size of institutions is a secondary problem. We must also accept that some facets of our current system are here to stay. Shrinking the financial sector will be slow going, so we're best off watching it more closely, forcing institutions to put stronger safety nets in place, and, most important, helping them fail gracefully when they make mistakes.

The logic behind "too big to fail" is that if a large financial firm or corporation goes under, it can drag along not just its own investors, creditors, and employees but also entire industries. But it's not merely a question of size. Neither Lehman Brothers nor Bear Stearns were among the largest banks in terms of assets, but their roles in the market gave their troubles an outsize negative effect on the broader economy. In other words, when we say "too big to fail," what we actually mean is "systemically risky" for any number of different reasons.

"It's just so nice and simple to say, 'If it's too big to fail, why don't we just keep them from getting big?'" says Diana Farrell, a top White House official working on financial regulation. She points out that some Japanese and European institutions are much larger than their U.S. counterparts, suggesting that size alone does not explain risk. "Let's recognize we live in a sophisticated economy that is going to require large, interconnected, complex firms. Let's make sure that we recognize them, ensure they do not pose a risk to the system," and guarantee they follow stricter rules.

The Obama administration's plan to restructure the financial system, which is wending its way through Congress, has sparked a complex battle between political parties, consumers, and industry stakeholders. At press time, the legislation included powerful changes like establishing a Consumer Financial Protection Agency, but its approach to systemic risk has come under fire because it appears to enshrine the problem, not solve it.

The administration proposes rearranging the regulatory system so that most national banks are under one supervisor, while the Federal Reserve and a council of regulators monitor risk throughout the system. Any institution—bank or not—

Essential Role of Big Banks

There are actually several good arguments for why the government's stepping in to preserve large private banks is a good idea. . . .

1. *Big banks finance risk-takers.* The U.S. economy needs risk-takers to provide financial services to the majority of citizens and businesses who are risk averse. . . .

2. *Big banks finance deals, especially big ones.* Large-scale mergers and acquisitions, as well as transactions involving private equity funds, normally require financing packages that are arranged in advance with complete secrecy. . . .

3. *Big banks can trade in size in global capital markets.* . . . Only large banking institutions can maintain ongoing relationships with giant counterparties, including multinational corporations, central banks or other government agencies, and sovereign wealth funds. . . .

4. *Big banks are in the derivatives business, small and medium-sized institutions are not.* Admittedly, this does not sound like a recommendation, given how many large financial institutions have gotten in trouble recently through mismanagement of their derivatives units. But derivatives are not going away. . . .

The above points explain why financial institutions grew so large and why that was and remains a generally good thing for the economy as a whole.

Roger M. Kubarych, Foreign Affairs, *June 17, 2009.*

that becomes systemically risky will be regulated by the Fed and subject to higher standards of capital, liquidity, and leverage. In theory, this will make large institutions less likely to fail and also encourage them to shrink themselves, because higher regulatory standards will hurt their bottom lines by putting a price on the public consequences of their systemic risk. Other reforms—to compensation structures, derivatives trading, and rating agencies—are designed to provide more information to regulators and better incentives to the market in order to complement efforts to control systemic risk. Equally important, the Fed will be able to observe all of the institution's activities as well as those of its subsidiaries. No more surprises, like the discovery that AIG was connected to almost every other major financial institution in the world.

"That does what we were unable to do in the case of AIG ... which is to provide the regulator a fully consolidated view of all activities, whether in the U.S. or otherwise, whether a depository institution or otherwise," Farrell says. "That itself becomes one of the critical prevention tools for systemic failure."

Those rules will be backstopped by a requirement that institutions keep an up-to-date scheme—a funeral plan—for how to wind down their operations in the event of failure. Most important, there will be new legal mechanisms, called "resolution authority," that regulators can use to shut down financial institutions while avoiding protracted bankruptcy during a crisis. Resolution authority will give the FDIC the power to do what it does best—arrange for the orderly liquidation of not only small banks but also big, international financial institutions.

"Being among the largest, most interconnected firms does not come with any guarantee of support in times of stress," Deputy Treasury Secretary Neal Wolin told a room full of bankers in September. "The presumption should be the opposite: Shareholders and creditors should expect to bear the costs of failure. . . . The resolution authority . . . allows the government to impose losses on shareholders and creditors without exposing the system to a sudden, disorderly failure that puts everyone else at risk."

But some critics warn that by designating more firms as systemically important, the government is implicitly guaranteeing prevention of their failure—and therefore broadening the amount of public money at risk. These critics want the administration to limit federal oversight to commercial banks and bar them from speculating in the markets or running investment funds that might put depositors at risk. While that is a good idea, the problem is, time and time again, institutions that aren't banks have found ways to engage in banking. Failing to include them in systemic risk regulation would be willfully blind. Regulation needs to be based on the principle that if it quacks like a bank, it should be treated like a bank.

The danger in the Obama administration's plan is that regulators, who are often too close to the banks, may not have the courage required to seize a failing institution—it might always be easier to fund the bankers through another bailout. One simple solution to this problem would be to eliminate regulators' ability to provide capital for banks or guarantee their liabilities, making liquidation the only option. But that cuts down on regulatory flexibility and is strongly opposed in the Treasury Department.

Within the FDIC, there is support for letting the systemic-risk exception apply only to markets, so that any costly measures in extremis will not benefit specific institutions. Perhaps the kind of restrictions that progressives wanted to put on the initial bailout loans—strict compensation limits, firing existing management, and even more stringent rules—should be codified so they will be clear if and when bailouts are needed again. The goal would be to penalize executives, not institutions, so the people at banks have the incentive to perform.

Regulatory reform is not just about providing new structures and tools. Reform is also about putting in place politicians and regulators who are willing to take the banks to task. The administration's proposed approach to the problem of systemically risky institutions would require the secretary of the Treasury to green-light any response to their failure, whether that response is bankruptcy, government-assisted liquidation, or even another bailout. That means direct political accountability to the president instead of the "Republic of the Central Banker" that we saw in 2008 as the Fed single-handedly undertook massive efforts to protect the financial system without any checks on its power—or its spending.

Looking back on last fall's argument between Geithner and Bair over what to do about Wachovia, it's clear that Bair was right in principle—using federal money to keep bad banks alive isn't a good idea. Geithner was right in practice—letting another bank fail would have only intensified the financial panic at a time when the Fed didn't have the right tools to solve the problems further bank failures would cause. What we need is a rulebook that doesn't force regulators to choose between those two approaches. We need a system designed by someone like Tim Geithner—and run by someone like Sheila Bair.

> "Small-scale community banks, thrifts,
> and credit unions have the potential, if
> favored with appropriate public policy,
> to ameliorate many of the country's
> deepest [financial] problems."

Small Banks Can Help Solve the Banking Crisis

Phillip Longman and Ellen Seidman

Phillip Longman is Schwartz Senior Fellow at the New America Foundation, a centrist think tank. He is the author of numerous books, among them Best Care Anywhere, *and writes for several magazines and newspapers, including the* Atlantic Monthly, Financial Times, Washington Post, Wall Street Journal, New York Times Magazine, *and the* New Republic. *Ellen Seidman is a senior fellow at the New America Foundation and an executive vice president at Shorebank Corporation, a community development bank holding company.*

In the following viewpoint Longman and Seidman rebut the theory that bigger is better when it comes to banks. Citing statistics that show that smaller banks have weathered the financial crisis better than their larger counterparts, they make the case

Phillip Longman and Ellen Seidman, "To Save America's Finances, Bring Back Community Banking," the New America Foundation Web site, November 20, 2008. Reproduced by permission.

for a Community Banking Trust Fund. The fund would enable community banks to increase lending to local businesses and homeowners. Because of the relationship these smaller banks have with their communities, they know the people and businesses they are lending to and are better able to judge risk than larger banks, the authors contend. Community banks also have a vested interest in fostering the growth and prosperity of the communities in which they reside, the authors note.

As you read, consider the following questions:

1. What two issues facing community banks do the authors believe could be helped through the creation of a Community Banking Trust Fund?

2. What two facts surrounding the credit crisis do Longman and Seidman cite to support their position that bigger banks were more culpable than smaller banks in creating the crisis?

3. How do the authors propose paying for the trust fund?

So far this year [in November 2008], the failure rate among big banks is seven times greater than among small banks. The latest available FDIC [Federal Deposit Insurance Corporation] data show that banks with less than $1 billion in assets are outperforming their larger peers with respect to the critical metrics of return on assets, net interest margin, and the all-important net charge-offs to loans and leases. While banks with between $100 million and $1 billion in assets charged off 0.37 percent of loans and leases, those with over $1 billion in assets charged off 1.35 percent.

Once regarded as at best niche, and at worst vestigial, players in a new world of global consumer finance, small-scale community banks, thrifts, and credit unions have the potential, if favored with appropriate public policy, to ameliorate many of the country's deepest problems. These include a dangerously high level of concentration within the financial services industry—a problem made especially acute as the Treasury rescue package allows big banks to get bigger. The promotion of small-scale banking can also help to improve the nonexistent savings rate, high consumer debt levels, and dwindling supplies of social capital in many areas. Finally, increasing the number and health of small-scale financial institutions can also help to overcome the lack of mutual interest between borrowers and lenders that is at the heart of the current global financial crisis.

Community banks and credit unions don't need a bailout, but they could use some help to deal with two major issues: the high fixed costs of some business essentials (such as information technology and meeting regulatory compliance costs) and access to capital, especially patient capital that will support them as they serve communities that now, more than ever, need both a place to save and access to responsible credit. We propose a Community Banking Trust Fund to respond to these needs.

The proposed fund would make equity investments in small-scale depository institutions that need patient capital to serve their communities effectively. For credit unions and mutually owned banks that do not issue stock, the fund would provide net worth certificates, which would count as equity, but pay a set interest rate. In addition, the fund would make technical assistance grants to cover critical investments in areas such as information technology and disaster recovery.

The fund would encourage these institutions to offer financial services that are limited in many communities, such as lending to local businesses and homeowners, safe and convenient mechanisms for savings, and transactional, cash management and investment services. Eligibility would be limited to banks, thrifts, and credit unions with a record of service to their communities as measured by high loan-to-deposit ratios, a high level of local lending, local deposits, local boards of directors, and high ratings under the Community Reinvestment Act.

We propose to start the fund with a one-time infusion of $30 billion from the $700 Treasury rescue package—an amount proportional to that which the Treasury has announced it will invest in the biggest banks. On an ongoing basis, the fund would be paid for through a tax of no more than 0.5 percent of the amount of newly issued asset-backed securities[1] —the very type of derivatives[2] that have been at the core of the current financial crisis.

Why Size Matters

A long dominant theory has held that when it comes to finance bigger is better. According to the theory, large financial institutions are more efficient due to their economies of scale and, more importantly, because of their ability to match lenders and borrowers wherever they might be around the world. Banks with global reach can take capital from wherever it is in oversupply (say, China or the United Arab Emirates) and direct it to places where it is in undersupply, no matter how distant (say, Stockton, California, or East Cleveland, Ohio). . . .

With the benefit of hindsight, however, we can see two clear facts that call into question whether global-scale finance really is more efficient than small-scale banking. First, the new system invested the world's savings in a spectacularly irrational manner. The money that poured into underwriting mortgages on McMansions and tract houses in automobile-dependent, jobless suburbs, it is now obvious, could have been more profitably invested in just about anything else—in, for example, rebuilding America's crumbling infrastructure, con-

---

1. A security is an investment instrument issued by a corporation, government, or other organization (excluding insurance policies and fixed annuities) that represents financial value. Securities can be debt (such as banknotes or bonds), equity (such as stocks), or derivatives (such as futures, options, or swaps).
2. A derivative is a financial instrument whose value is derived from an underlying asset, index, event, value, or condition. The derivative itself is merely a contract to exchange cash or assets over time based on fluctuations in the underlying assets. Most derivatives are characterized by high leverage, or debt.

verting to sustainable energy sources, or constructing affordable rental housing near good jobs and schools.

In contrast, small-scale financial institutions generally avoided subprime[3] lending and related derivatives, concentrated on traditional mortgage and small business loans, and today are in comparatively good shape. Though vulnerable to a downturn in the economy, with few exceptions they appear to be resistant to the financial contagion striking down larger institutions. So is bigger really better?

The second clear fact that emerges with hindsight is that it was the lack of a relationship of mutual interest between lender and borrower that was at the heart of the breakdown in global finance. All the different players in the system, from mortgage brokers to investment banks peddling "asset"-backed securities had little interest in whether consumers could actually afford their debt.

Unlike a traditional community bank, for example, few lenders held on to even some of the mortgages they wrote. Nor did they depend on deposits from the same people to whom they made loans. Instead, most of their money was made on fees. When faraway funding sources without any understanding of who or what they're funding substitute for local depositors, when loans can be sold without effective recourse, when borrowers are told not to worry about repayment because never-ending refinancing will be available, everyone loses.

In traditional small-scale banking, by contrast, there is a mutuality of interest between borrower and lender. This mutuality has both a soft and a hard side. On the soft side, small-scale banking means that savers, borrowers, and lenders all have a heightened ability to judge each other's character and to hold each other accountable. They are all members of a

3. Subprime mortgages are those to individuals with poor credit histories who would not be able to qualify for conventional mortgages. Higher interest rates are charged on subprime mortgages than on conventional mortgages because of the increased risk of default for lenders.

A Letter to Congress

The Independent Community Bankers of America on behalf of its 5,000 community bank members throughout the country, urges you to cosponsor H.R. 2897, the Bank Accountability and Risk Assessment Act of 2009, by Rep. [Luis] Gutierrez. H.R. 2897 makes the too-big-too-fail banks accountable to taxpayers and the FDIC [Federal Deposit Insurance Corporation] for the risk that their operations represent.

Independent Community Bankers of America,
Letter to U.S. Representatives, July 10, 2009.

community and, as such, subject to social pressures to act responsibly. George Bailey [the main character in film *It's a Wonderful Life*] didn't write loans containing improvised explosive devices in part because he saw his customers regularly around Bedford Falls and knew his thrift's business depended on his good reputation. His customers, in turn, would face the opprobrium [scorn] of their neighbors if they walked away from their loans.

In small-scale banking, borrowers and lenders also know each other's prospects better than borrowers and lenders on opposite sides of globe. Put another way, small-scale banks are rich with what Federal Reserve Chairman Ben Bernanke calls "informational capital," which they develop through "gathering relevant information, as well as by maintaining ongoing relationships with customers." . . .

Policy Levers

What policy levers are available to encourage the growth of responsible, small-scale financial institutions? One, obviously, is continued regulatory crackdown on predatory lenders. Close the predators down, and more space will be created for traditional financial institutions dedicated to thrift and mutuality of interest. When Washington, D.C., finally shut down payday lending, local credit unions saw an upsurge in business.

The creation of national standards for mortgages, credit card contracts, and other loan products would also help level the playing field between responsible and irresponsible lenders. . . .

To increase the number of small-scale financial institutions, we have to address their biggest challenge, which is access to patient capital. They need funds that can be leveraged eight or ten times over to make good loans in the community—at rates and terms that generate a reasonable, if not a spectacular, rate of return. Badly burned by losses on Wall Street and their experience with exploding mortgages, many Americans are already redirecting their savings to insured deposits and seeking as well to forge a personal relationship with their bankers—trends that bode well for community banking. Still, a robust community banking sector requires funding beyond local deposits. . . .

There are essentially five ways a bank or credit union can expand its ability to lend funds beyond those provided by local customer deposits: raising deposits outside the local area, borrowing against assets (using the loans it holds as collateral), selling loans, earning income from other sources such as fees, and raising more equity capital from investors. A major challenge facing community banks is whether they can access these sources while retaining their community connection. . . .

The biggest problem facing small banks today, however, is attracting long-term equity capital from stockholders. Most small banks are privately held, and even for those that are not, interesting the public in banks stocks is not easy. This problem could get worse for small banks if, after all the bailouts, just a few giant financial institutions control most banking. This outcome now seems more likely, especially since it has become government policy, under the Treasury's Troubled Asset Relief Program (TARP), to favor large institutions with the lion's share of equity infusions.

Small banks have always needed a proportionately higher level of equity because of their higher cost structure, their lack of diversification, and (for the majority that are either mutually owned or closely held) their lack of easy access to the capital markets. In the current market environment, particularly with reduced access to loan sales, community banks and credit unions that want to step up their lending need sources of additional capital. Equity is important both as a risk cushion and as the basis for leverage. Even conservative small banks leverage[4] each dollar of equity into about $7 of loans. For community banks serving low-income areas, accessing additional capital can be particularly difficult, but the additional opportunity to lend generated by the equity is especially important.

A Community Banking Trust Fund

To solve these obstacles to greater mutuality of interest between borrowers and lenders, we propose the establishment of a Community Banking Trust Fund. As previously stated, the fund would make equity investments in small-scale depository institutions that need patient equity capital to serve their communities effectively. In addition, the fund would make nontaxable technical assistance grants to cover critical investments in such areas as information technology and disaster recovery. . . .

Only banks and credit unions that won formal designation as community banks or credit unions would be eligible to participate in the Community Banking Trust Fund. Currently, "community bank" is an industry term that has no specific legal definition. Generally, it refers to smaller, local banks that concentrate on personal service. Some cater principally to up-

4. Leverage is the use of debt to grow an investment.

scale citizens and small business owners who demand personal attention. Others, typically known as community development banks, have social missions and are deeply involved in local community building efforts. But there are also banks with as much as several billion dollars in assets and far-flung branch networks that call themselves community banks. Some of these, especially those made up of formerly independent banks that retain their identity, still are. Others use the moniker mainly because they once were community banks and the phrase has a nice ring to it.

Under our proposal, to become a federally designated community bank or credit union, and therefore eligible for equity investment from the Community Banking Trust Fund, an institution would have to remain small. We define small as holding assets of no more than $5 billion. Participating institutions would also be required to seek out local deposits, and concentrate the vast bulk of their lending (say, 70 percent) on home mortgages, multi-family mortgages, and consumer, business (including nonprofit), and local government loans within a limited geographic area.

They would also have to show demonstrable investment in their local community through high loan-to-deposit ratios, coupled with a high market share of local depositors (taking into account the ability of the community to provide deposits). That means service to the entire community, including minorities, immigrants, and those of modest means. No country club banks need apply. Other criteria would include having board members who are of the community and the performance of community service by officers and employees of the bank. . . .

Funding

How much money are we talking about? The Treasury Department has announced that it will invest up to $250 billion in preferred stock in banks and thrifts, at the rate of between

1 percent and 3 percent of an institution's risk-weighted assets. (This is the dollar amount of assets such as loans, increased or decreased according to regulatory standards to reflect their riskiness.)

As of June 30, 2008, total risk-weighted assets of banks and thrifts with under $1 billion in assets were about $1.1 trillion. Thus, banks and thrifts of this size could conceivably receive between $11 billion and $33 billion from the Treasury's program. As of June 30, 2008, the assets of all credit unions totaled $740 billion, with $328 billion of that in credit unions under $500 million in assets. Using the same analysis, if credit unions were eligible for the Treasury program, their share would be between $7 billion and $21 billion. In comparison, each of several large banks got infusions of $25 billion. . . .

How much would this cost on an ongoing basis? The needed level of support can only be approximated. As discussed above, most small institutions are doing well. But let's assume that each year the group in the aggregate would need about one-half of 1 percent of assets to ensure its continued ability to meet community needs. Assuming take-up rates remain constant, that works out to a total annual cost of about $7 billion.

Where would this funding (as well a much smaller amount for grants for technology upgrades and similar needs) come from? We propose that on an ongoing basis, the funding for both equity and grants come from a tax on securitized loan transactions, which are the type of transactions that have the least mutuality between borrower and funder, the lack of which led to the current crisis. . . .

Virtues of Small Banks

As we foster small-scale banking we must avoid past regulatory errors, such as the infamous Regulation Q that prevented thrifts and commercial banks from paying market rates for deposits and led to the savings and loan crisis [in the early

1990s]. Too much coddling and protection for small-scale bankers could also erode their competitiveness and spirit of enterprise, which became a big problem in the 1960s and 1970s, and remains so to a lesser extent today. More community bankers need to learn to apply information technology, which fortunately is becoming more affordable, to lower the cost of their operations and transactions.

At the end of the day, it is also clear that small-scale banking won't work unless Americans regain the savings habit. Such a change in behavior will have to happen in any event, as rapid population aging in creditor nations, unsustainable trade imbalances, and other factors reduce the amount of foreign capital Americans can cheaply import. Moreover, small-scale banks can help to foster a return to the thrift ethos. They can do this by bringing back banking and credit union services to areas where residents are currently "unbanked" and by promoting financial education and thrift.

A final argument for encouraging small-scale banking looks to the near future. The ongoing credit crisis had its roots in the destruction of the mutuality of interest between borrowers and lenders. That mutuality is now becoming further eroded by the even greater consolidation of financial services institutions that is emerging from the crisis itself. By the fall of 2008, just three institutions, Citigroup, Bank of America, and JPMorgan Chase, held more than 30 percent of the nation's deposits, while also holding 40 percent of bank loans to corporations. We should not be surprised if large banks wind up using much of the public money they are now receiving to buy up smaller banks. When the credit crisis is past, just a handful of "banks," for want of a better term for these hydra-headed goliaths, will control most of the market.

Our proposal for a Community Banking Trust Fund will cost money. But funding will come by taxing, and therefore discouraging, those forms of transactional, securitized borrowing that led to the current crisis. Moreover, making the

Community Banking Trust Fund part of our new regulatory architecture will help redress the long-term distortions caused by the massive federal investments now flowing from the Treasury to big banks—some of them the very institutions responsible for our current troubles.

Since the Progressive Era [1890s to 1920s] and before, community banks, thrifts, and credit unions have served customers in a manner that promoted mutuality while also serving as a check against monopoly finance in the hands of a few money-center banks. Before the conflagration of the global financial system brought on by predatory subprime mortgage lending practices and other irrational uses of the world's savings, singing the virtues of small-scale banks might have seemed nostalgic and romantic. After the painful bursting of three financial bubbles in a decade, however, paying attention to those virtues is both essential and hardheaded.

In *It's a Wonderful Life*, George Bailey got to see how much poorer his world would be if he hadn't existed. Today, a world that has passed him by looks ugly indeed.

"*Our goal is to help ensure that there is a much closer alignment between compensation, sound risk management and long-term value creation for firms and the economy as a whole.*"

Executive Compensation of Bankers Needs to Be Fixed

Gene Sperling

Gene Sperling, an American economist, spoke before the House Financial Services Committee on the topic of executive compensation in his role as counselor to treasury secretary Timothy Geithner. Sperling is also a senior fellow for economic policy and director of the Center for Universal Education at the Council on Foreign Affairs. He was director of the National Economic Council in the Bill Clinton administration from 1996 to 2000 and is the author of The Pro-Growth Progressive.

Sperling maintains in the following viewpoint that a significant factor contributing to the financial crisis was executive compensation practices that were based on short-term results and that encouraged actions that had long-term risks. He recommends several reforms to more closely align compensation with effective risk management and long-term value creation.

Gene Sperling, "Gene Sperling's Testimony on Compensation," testimony to the House Financial Services Committee, June 11, 2009.

As you read, consider the following questions:

1. What are the performance metrics that the author recommends be considered when setting executive compensation plans?

2. What is a mechanism that Sperling suggests can be used to align compensation with long-term value creation?

3. What is a mechanism that the author suggests can be utilized to minimize long-term risk?

Each of us involved in economic policy has an obligation to fully understand the factors that contributed to this financial crisis and to make our best effort to find the policies that minimize the likelihood of its recurrence. There is little question that one contributing factor to the excessive risk taking that was central to the crisis was the prevalence of compensation practices at financial institutions that encouraged short-term gains to be realized with little regard to the potential economic damage such behavior could cause not only to those firms, but to the financial system and economy as a whole. As [treasury] Secretary [Timothy] Geithner said yesterday [June 10, 2009], too often "incentives for short-term gains overwhelmed the checks and balances meant to mitigate against the risk of excess leverage."[1]

Compensation structures that permitted key executives and other financial actors to avoid the potential long-term downsides of their actions discouraged a focus on determining long-term risk and underlying economic value, while reducing the number of financial market participants with an incentive to be a "canary in the coal mine."

The Role of Compensation

After one large investment bank suffered large losses, it acknowledged—properly reflecting on what it should have done

1. Leverage is the use of debt to grow an investment.

differently—that it had skewed its employees' incentives by simply measuring bonuses against gross revenue after personnel costs, with "no formal account taken of the quality or sustainability of those earnings." And the potential harm caused by compensation arrangements based on short-term results with little account for long-term risks went beyond top executives. Indeed, across the subprime[2] mortgage industry, brokers were often compensated in ways that placed a high premium on the volume of their lending without regard to whether borrowers had the ability to make their payments. As a result, lenders, whose compensation normally did not require them to internalize long-term risk, had a strong incentive to increase volume by targeting riskier and riskier borrowers—and they did, contributing to the problems that spurred our current crisis.

As we work to restore financial stability, the focus on executive compensation at companies that have received governmental assistance is appropriate and understandable. But what is most important for our economy at large is the topic of this hearing: understanding how compensation practices contributed to this financial crisis and what steps we can take to ensure they do not cause excessive risk-taking in the future. And while the financial sector has been at the center of this issue, we believe that compensation practices must be better aligned with long-term value and prudent risk management at all firms, and not just for the financial services industry.

Yesterday Secretary Geithner laid out a set of principles for moving forward with compensation reforms. Our goal is to help ensure that there is a much closer alignment between compensation, sound risk management and long-term value creation for firms and the economy as a whole. Our goal is not to have the government micromanage private sector com-

2. Subprime mortgages are those granted to individuals with poor credit histories who would not be able to qualify for conventional mortgages. Higher interest rates are charged on subprime mortgages than conventional mortgages because of the increased risk of default for lenders.

pensation. As Secretary Geithner said yesterday, "We are not capping pay. We are not setting forth precise prescriptions for how companies should set compensation, which can often be counterproductive." We also recognize these principles may evolve over time, and we look forward to engaging in a discussion with this Committee [House Financial Services Committee], the Congress, supervisors, academics and other compensation experts, shareholders and the business community about the best path. We begin this conversation recognizing that the reforms we put in place must be based not only on our best intentions, but also a clear-eyed understanding of the need to minimize unintended consequences. But we think these principles offer a promising way forward.

Compensation Tied to Performance

There is little debate that compensation should be tied to performance in order to best align the incentives of executives with those of shareholders. But even compensation that is nominally performance-based has often rewarded failure or set benchmarks too low to have a meaningful impact.

There is increasing consensus in the expert community that performance-based compensation must involve a thoughtful combination of metrics that is indexed to relative performance as opposed to just following the ups and downs of the market. Performance pay based solely on stock price can on the one hand, "confuse brains for a bull-market" and in the other scenario, fail to recognize exceptional contributions by executives in difficult times. A thoughtful mix of performance metrics could include not only stock prices, but individual performance assessments, adherence to risk management and measures that account for the long-term soundness of the firm.

Compensation Structure

As I mention above, much of the damage caused by this crisis occurred when people were able to capture excessive and im-

Compensation Not Tied to Results

There is no clear rhyme or reason to the way banks compensate and reward their employees. In many ways, the past three years [2006–2009] have provided a virtual laboratory in which to test the hypothesis that compensation in the financial industry was performance-based. But even a cursory examination of the data suggests that in these challenging economic times, compensation for bank employees has become unmoored from the banks' financial performance.

Thus, when the banks did well, their employees were paid well. When the banks did poorly, their employees were paid well. And when the banks did very poorly, they were bailed out by taxpayers and their employees were still paid well. Bonuses and overall compensation did not vary significantly as profits diminished.

Andrew M. Cuomo,
Bank Bonus Report, *July 30, 2009.*

mediate gains without their compensation reflecting the long-term risks they were imposing on their companies, their shareholders, and ultimately, the economy as a whole. Financial firms offered incentives to invest heavily in complex financial instruments that yielded large gains in the short-term, but presented a "tail risk" of major losses. Inevitably, these practices contributed to an overwhelming focus on gains—as they allowed the payout of significant amounts of compensation today without any regard for the possible downside that might come tomorrow.

That is why we believe companies should seek to pay both executives and other employees in ways that are tightly aligned with the long-term value and soundness of the firm. One traditional way of doing so is to provide compensation for executives overwhelmingly in stock that must be held for a long period of time—even beyond retirement. Such compensation structures also reduce the risk that executives might walk away with large pay packages in one year only to see their firms crumble in the next year or two. In these cases, the dramatic decline in stock price would effectively "claw back" the previous year's pay. Other firms keep bonuses "at risk," so that if large profits in one year are followed by poor performance in the next, the bonuses will be reduced. . . .

Fostering Sound Risk Management

Ensuring that compensation fosters sound risk-management requires pay strategies that do not allow market participants to completely externalize their long-term risk, while also ensuring that those responsible for risk management receive the compensation and the authority within firms to provide a check on excessive risk-taking. As the Financial Stability Forum recently stated, "staff engaged in financial and risk control must be independent, have appropriate authority, and be compensated in a manner that is independent of the business areas they oversee and commensurate with their key role in the firm."

This authority and independence is all the more important in times of excessive optimism when consistent—though unsustainable—asset appreciation can temporarily make the reckless look wise and the prudent look overly risk-averse. Former Federal Reserve Chairman William McChesney Martin Jr. once said that "The job of the Federal Reserve is to take away the punch bowl just when the party starts getting interesting." Likewise, risk managers must have the independence, stature and pay to take the car keys away when they believe a temporary good-time may be creating even a small risk of a major financial accident down the road.

Yet there are several reports showing the degree to which risk managers lacked the appropriate authority during the run-up to this financial crisis. Accounts of one Wall Street firm discuss how risk managers who once roamed the trading floors to gain a better understanding of how the company worked and where weaknesses might exist were denied access to that necessary information and discouraged from expressing their concerns.

That is why we believe that compensation committees should conduct and publish a risk assessment of whether pay structures—not only for top executives, but for all employees—incentivize excessive risk-taking. As part of this process, committees should identify whether an employee or executive experiences a penalty if their exceptional performance is based on decisions that ultimately put the long-term health of the firm in danger. At the same time, managers should also have direct reporting access to the compensation committee to enhance their impact. . . .

Golden Parachutes

While golden parachutes [guarantees of large severance packages] were created to align executives' interests with those of shareholders during mergers, they have expanded in ways that may not be consistent with the long-term value of the firm, and—as of 2006—were in place at over 80 percent of the largest firms. Likewise, supplemental retirement packages that are intended to provide financial security to employees are too often used to obscure the full amount of "walkaway" pay due a top executive once they leave the firm. Indeed, [Harvard professors] Lucian Bebchuk and Jesse Fried have shown that there is substantial evidence that "firms use retirement benefits to provide executives with substantial amounts of 'stealth compensation'—compensation not transparent to shareholders—that is largely decoupled from performance."

Examining these practices is all the more important because when workers who are losing their jobs see the top executives at their firms walking away with huge severance packages, it creates the understandable impression that there is a double-standard in which top executives are rewarded for failure at the same time working families are forced to sacrifice. As Secretary Geithner said yesterday, "we should reexamine how well these golden parachutes and supplemental retirement packages are aligned with shareholder interests, whether they truly incentivize performance and whether they reward top executives even if their shareholders lose value."

Promote Transparency

Many of the excessive compensation practices in place during the financial crisis likely would have been discouraged or reexamined if they had been implemented by truly independent compensation committees and were transparent to a company's owners—its shareholders. Companies often hire compensation consultants who also provide the firm millions of dollars in other services—creating conflicts of interest. According to one Congressional investigation, the median CEO [chief executive officer] salary of Fortune 250 companies in 2006 that hired compensation consultants with the largest conflicts of interest was 67 percent higher than the median CEO salary of the companies that did not use consultants with such conflicts of interest.

That is why we hope to work with Chairman [Barney] Frank and this committee to pass "say on pay" legislation, requiring all public companies to hold a non-binding shareholder resolution to approve executive compensation packages. We believe that "say on pay" will place a greater check on boards to ensure that their compensation packages are aligned with the interest of shareholders. . . .

As we move to repair our financial system, get our economy growing again and pursue a broad agenda of regulatory reform, we must ensure that the compensation practices that contributed to this crisis no longer put our system and our economy at risk. I commend the committee for holding these hearings, and I look forward to approaching this difficult issue with a degree of seriousness, reflection and humility—seriousness over the harm excessive risk-taking has caused for so many innocent people; reflection over the lessons we have already learned; and humility in recognizing the complexity of this issue, its potential for unintended consequences, and the importance of testing each of our ideas against the most rigorous analysis.

> "Properly designed capital requirements
> are a much more efficient approach to
> regulate the risk of financial institu-
> tions than fiddling with compensation."

Regulating Executive Compensation Will Not Solve the Banking Problem

Floyd Norris

Floyd Norris is chief financial correspondent of the New York
Times. *With his wife, Christine Bockelmann, he compiled and
edited* The New York Times Century of Business.

*Although many are outraged by bankers' compensation pack-
ages, these packages were not responsible for the financial crisis
and regulating them will not solve it, argues Norris in the following viewpoint. He cites as evidence for his position a study
showing that banking chief executive officers with significant
stock typically ran banks that fared worse than other banks during the crisis. He contends that these chief executives were highly
motivated for their institutions to do well. That they did not
perform well is due to the executives' failure to understand the*

level of risk present in the economy, a failure that was widespread in the economic community, and not due to compensation practices.

As you read, consider the following questions:

1. How does the author characterize the effectiveness of Congress's last attempt at regulating executive pay?

2. According to Norris, what is the theory of "Great Moderation"?

3. As cited by the author, what were Richard Fuld's stock and option holdings worth at one time and what are they currently worth?

There is a lot about Wall Street pay to make the rest of us livid, or at least jealous. And now Congress seems poised to act on it.

The House of Representatives is expected to pass on Friday [July 31, 2009,] a bill to empower regulators to change what the bill's sponsor, Barney Frank, calls "imprudently risky compensation practices" on Wall Street.

Other companies will have to face regular shareholder votes on pay, although the votes will be nonbinding, and board compensation committees will have to jump through more hoops.

The big winners will be compensation consultants, for whom there are likely to be more jobs available as conflicts of interest force companies to hire more consultants.

I doubt all of this will hurt very much, unlike the last Congressional stab at doing something about excessive executive pay, passed when Jimmy Carter was president. That led to soaring pay and some of the abuses that now outrage people.

But neither will it do much good.

Failure to Understand Risk

It is galling to see executives making tens of millions of dollars for running companies that have to be bailed out by taxpayers, but there is little evidence that big pay—or the incentives connected to it—caused the financial train wreck that sent the world into recession.

To the contrary, there is plenty of evidence that no one who counted—traders, chief executives or regulators—understood the risks that were being taken.

A new study shows that banks run by chief executives with a lot of stock were, if anything, likely to do worse than other banks in the crisis.

"Bank C.E.O. [chief executive officer] incentives cannot be blamed for the credit crisis or for the performance of banks during the crisis," states the study, by René Stulz, an Ohio State University finance professor, and Rüdiger Fahlenbrach of the Swiss Federal Institute of Technology.

"A plausible explanation for these findings is that C.E.O.'s focused on the interests of their shareholders in the build-up to the crisis and took actions that they believed the market would welcome," Mr. Stulz said.

The chief executives were wrong, of course. Most lost tens of millions of dollars in equity value but sold few shares before the crisis hit.

Whatever else they lacked, they had plenty of incentive to keep their banks from failing.

But those incentives did not matter when they should have. Bankers and regulators believed in the "Great Moderation," a term popularized by Ben Bernanke, then a member and now the chairman of the Federal Reserve Board, in a 2004 speech.

Thanks in part to "improvements in monetary policy," Mr. Bernanke said, without excessive modesty, there had been "a reduction in the extent of economic uncertainty confronting households and firms." Recessions, he added, "have become less frequent and less severe."

Bankers were not the only ones who concluded that the chances of a very bad outcome were exceedingly low. As year after year went by with nothing very bad happening, they saw no reason not to borrow more and more money to place what they deemed to be safe bets.

It may be worth noting that, of the 98 financial companies studied by Professors Stulz and Fahlenbrach, the one with the most valuable holdings of stock and options in his company at the end of 2006 was Richard Fuld of Lehman Brothers. His holdings, now worthless, were valued at $1 billion.

I had lunch with Mr. Fuld in early 2008, after the financial crisis was under way and less than eight months before Lehman failed. The conversation was off the record, but I am sure he had no inkling of how great were the risks Lehman faced as a leader in the mortgage securitization[1] business.

He was later raked over the coals in Congressional hearings about his huge compensation. That most of it was in stock and options that he never cashed in seemed to be something most legislators could not comprehend.

As Congress moves to do something about executive pay, it is worth asking what would have happened if Mr. Fuld had somehow realized in 2005 that the mortgage business was a time bomb and had gotten Lehman out of it. Within a year, its profits would have sagged and its share price collapsed. Mr. Fuld would have been labeled a dunce, and might have lost his job. The same can be said of Jimmy Cayne of Bear Stearns and Stan O'Neal of Merrill Lynch, the two runners-up in the richest bank C.E.O. sweepstakes of 2006.

President [Barack] Obama has proposed legislation to deal with many aspects of the financial crisis, and it is no surprise

1. Securitization is the process of aggregating similar types of investments, typically loans or mortgages, into a common pool, then selling that pool of investments.

No Solution

Americans are understandably disturbed when taxpayer-supported companies pay outsized bonuses. But government regulation of private-sector pay is no solution. Existing tax law encourages excessive focus on executive bonuses. Additional government intervention will imbalance corporate governance and further distort pay practices.

Rather than dictating private-sector pay, policymakers should re-examine the pernicious effects of existing tax incentives on executive pay.

David M. Mason, Heritage Foundation
WebMemo, No 2570, July 30, 2009.

that this bill is the one that seems to be having the easiest road to passage, even though every Republican voted against it in the House Financial Services Committee. The banks probably realize it won't make much difference and are doing their most intensive lobbying elsewhere.

I asked Professor Stulz what he thought of the bill. "It is hard to believe that regulators will be better at devising compensation plans with proper incentives," he said. "Properly designed capital requirements are a much more efficient approach to regulate the risk of financial institutions than fiddling with compensation."

Indeed, much of the financial "innovation" of recent years consisted of bankers coming up with ways to evade capital requirements. The regulators are now trying to deal with that, but their efforts are handicapped by bankers warning that they will maker fewer loans if capital rules are tightened.

Bill May Have Some Benefits

That said, the bill could help some. The Sarbanes-Oxley law[2], passed in 2002, does seem to have resulted in board audit committees taking their jobs much more seriously. It would be good if the same happened at compensation committees. Perhaps it will do some good to tie compensation to long-term results, or to force executives to hold stock rather than sell it quickly when options vest.

Still, as Alan Blinder, the Princeton economist and former vice chairman of the Fed, wrote recently in the *Wall Street Journal*: "The executives, lawyers and accountants who design compensation systems are imaginative, skilled and definitely not disinterested. Congress and government bureaucrats won't beat them at this game."

The last time Congress took action in response to populist outrage at executive pay, it changed tax laws to bar salaries of more than $1 million from being deducted as corporate expenses. Payments based on performance could still be deducted.

The result was not what Congress intended. At large companies, $1 million soon became a floor, not a ceiling, for the boss's salary. Bonus and stock option plans proliferated to take advantage of the "performance-based" loophole. Eventually, we got to the oxymoron of "guaranteed bonuses."

Since most of their promised compensation was in the form of bonuses, Wall Streeters could not understand why people thought they should not be paid just because their firms had to be bailed out. A promise is a promise, they said.

We can hope that this bill will have fewer unintended consequences. But even if Mr. Frank, the chairman of the House Financial Services Committee, is right to call it "the first step

2. The Sarbanes-Oxley Act was enacted following a number of corporate and accounting scandals in the early 2000s, and set more rigorous accounting standards for publicly traded companies.

towards comprehensive financial regulatory reform," there will have to be much larger steps taken to reach that goal.

Periodical Bibliography

The following articles have been selected to supplement the diverse views presented in this chapter.

Anders Aslund	"Rules for a Bank Bailout," *Washington Post*, February 6, 2009.
E.J. Dionne	"The Obama Enigma," *Real Clear Politics*, April 2, 2009.
Timothy Geithner	"My Plan for Bad Bank Assets," *Wall Street Journal*, March 23, 2009.
David C. John	"The Obama Financial Regulatory Plan: Poor Policy and Missed Opportunities," Heritage Foundation *WebMemo*, July 15, 2009.
Paul Krugman	"Banking on the Brink," *New York Times*, February 23, 2009.
Paul Krugman	"The Big Dither," *New York Times*, March 6, 2009.
Robert Kuttner	"Betting the Fed," *American Prospect*, June 1, 2009.
Robert Kuttner	"Slouching Towards Solvency," *American Prospect*, March 23, 2009.
Harold Meyerson	"The Nationalization Option," *Washington Post*, March 18, 2009.
Joe Nocera	"First, Let's Fix the Bonuses," *New York Times*, February 21, 2009.
Nomi Prins	"Risk Is Best Managed from the Bottom Up," *American Prospect*, May 6, 2009.
Stuart Rothenberg	"If This Is Bank Nationalization, It's Not What Marx Meant," *Real Clear Politics*, February 27, 2009.
James Surowiecki	"Balancing Banks," *New Yorker*, April 6, 2009.

CHAPTER 4

What Role Did Foreign Investment Play in the U.S. Banking Crisis?

Chapter Preface

The role that foreign investment in the United States played in the banking crisis is a matter of some debate. Former U.S. secretary of the treasury Henry Paulson has been a leading proponent of the theory that global economic imbalances, caused mainly by China, helped foster the credit crisis by pushing down interest rates and driving investors towards riskier assets.

This charge has been roundly denounced by Chinese officials, who instead lay the blame for the credit crisis on U.S. economic policy and the greed of the U.S. financial markets. Speaking in January 2009, Chinese premier Wen Jiabao stated responsibility for the crisis lay with the "inappropriate macroeconomic policies of some economies and their unsustainable model of development characterized by prolonged low savings and high consumption." He went on to cite "an excessive expansion of financial institutions in blind pursuit of profit, lack of self discipline among financial institutions and ratings agencies."

While there are varying views on the role Chinese investment played in causing the crisis, there is agreement that a Chinese–United States trade imbalance and the heavy investment of the Chinese in U.S. securities created a situation of risk. For a variety of reasons, the Chinese are a nation of savers. China's savings rate for consumers is 28 percent of their household income, while in the United States, the savings rate hit an all-time low of 0.5 pecent in 2005. It grew to 6.9 percent in May 2009, as wary Americans reacted to the recession by increasing their personal savings. The large United States–China trade deficit resulted from the fact that the United States imports far more Chinese products than the Chinese purchase from the United States. In 2008, the trade deficit was $268 billion. Complicating matters, lured by the opportunity to purchase safe, growing investments, China recycled its trade profits right back into the United States. In the decade ending in 2008, China invested $1 trillion in the United States, mostly in government bonds and mortgage debt guaranteed by the U.S. government.

As Mark Landler reported in the December 25, 2008, *New York Times*, "China kept its banks under tight state control and its currency on a short leash to ensure financial stability. It required companies and individuals to save in the state-run banking system most of the foreign currency—primarily dollars—that they earned from foreign trade and investment.

> As foreign trade surged, this hoard of dollars became enormous. In 2000, the reserves were less than $200 billion; today [in 2008] they are about $2 trillion.

> Chinese leaders chose to park the bulk of that in safe securities backed by the American government, including Treasury bonds and the debt of Fannie Mae and Freddie Mac, which had implicit government backing.

> This not only allowed the United States to continue to finance its trade deficit, but, by creating greater demand for United States securities, it also helped push interest rates below where they would otherwise have been.

As stated by Moritz Schularick, a visiting scholar at the University of Cambridge who teaches economics and economic history at the Free University of Berlin, in the February 24, 2009, *Financial Times*, "Beijing and others cannot be blamed for reckless lending into the housing bubble or leverage in western financial institutions, but it is clear that a vast amount of capital was flowing from a developing country with a per capita income of one tenth of the western world to one of the richest economies in the world. Water was flowing uphill in unprecedented amounts."

In the chapter that follows, the role of foreign investment in the United States as well as the role U.S. investment in offshore banking played in the crisis are debated.

"A Government Accountability Office report . . . found that 83 of the United States' top 100 companies operate subsidiaries in tax havens."

Foreign Tax Havens Contributed to the Banking Crisis

Rachel Keeler

Rachel Keeler is an international business journalist. She writes for a number of publications, including Financial Times *and* Ratio Magazine.

In the following viewpoint, Keeler describes the enormous amount of wealth that is sheltered from taxes in foreign tax havens, representing billions of dollars in lost tax revenues. She contends that the presence of these havens contributed to the financial crisis, as many of the most risky investment vehicles were housed offshore unencumbered by U.S. regulations. The crisis has had the effect of drawing international attention to the problem of tax havens, she explains, raising the hope that real reform will occur.

Rachel Keeler, "Tax Havens and the Financial Crisis," *Dollars & Sense: Real World Economics*, May/June 2009, pp. 21–25. Copyright © 2009 Economic Affairs Bureau, Inc. Reprinted by permission of Dollars and Sense, a progressive economics magazine (www.dollarsandsense.org).

As you read, consider the following questions:

1. What percent of the world's hedge funds are housed in the Caribbean, according to the author?

2. Which country is the world's largest tax haven and how much offshore money is located in its banks, as reported by Keeler?

3. In the US, when does tax avoidance become tax evasion, according to the author?

Over the years, trillions of dollars in both corporate profits and personal wealth have migrated "offshore" in search of rock bottom tax rates and the comfort of no questions asked. Tax havens and other financial centers promoting low tax rates, light regulation, and financial secrecy include a long list of tropical nations like the Cayman Islands as well as whole mainland economies from Switzerland to Singapore.

Nature of the Beast

Tax Justice Network, an international non-profit advocating tax haven reform, estimates one-third of global assets are held offshore. The offshore world harbors $11.5 trillion in individual wealth alone, representing $250 billion in lost annual tax revenue. Treasury figures show tax havens sucking $100 billion a year out of U.S. coffers. And these numbers have all been growing steadily over the past decade. A Tax Notes study found that between 1999 and 2002, the amount of profits U.S. companies reported in tax havens grew from $88 billion to $149 billion.

With little patience left for fat-cat tax scams, the public is finally cheering for reform. Tax havens, it seems, have become the perfect embodiment of suddenly unfashionable capitalist greed. Unemployed workers and unhappy investors grow hot with anger as they imagine exotic hideouts where businessmen go to sip poolside martinis and laugh off their national tax burden.

Reformers have tried and failed in the past to shut down these locales. But analysts say 2008, the year the global financial system finally collapsed under its own liberalized weight, made all the difference. Not only are governments now desperate for tax revenue to help fund bailouts, but a recognition of the role offshore financial centers played in the system's implosion is dawning. . . .

[Economists] and policymakers including Treasury Secretary Timothy Geithner have pointed to the shadow banking system[1] as a root cause of the global crisis. They're talking about the raft of highly-leveraged,[2] virtually unregulated investment vehicles developed over the last 20 years: hedge funds,[3] private equity,[4] conduits,[5] structured investment vehicles (SIVs),[6] collateralized debt obligations (CDOs),[7] and other wildly arcane investment banker toys.

While most of these innovations were born of Wall Street imaginations, few found their home in New York. Seventy-five percent of the world's hedge funds are based in four Caribbean tax havens: the Cayman Islands, Bermuda, the British Virgin Islands, and the Bahamas. The two subprime mortgage-

1. The shadow banking system consists of nonbank financial institutions, such as hedge funds, that act as intermediaries between investors and borrowers.
2. Leverage is the use of debt to grow an investment.
3. A hedge fund is a pooled private investment fund that seeks to maximize returns with strategies that include unconventional investments and investments that cannot quickly be converted to cash, such as real estate.
4. Private equity companies invest in companies that are not publicly traded on a stock exchange. Investments in private equity typically involve either the acquisition of an operating company or the investment of capital into an operating company.
5. Conduits are government or private organizations that assemble mortgages and other loans into a large pool, and issue securities in the name of the conduit to investors.
6. Structured investment vehicles are pools of investment assets that attempt to profit from credit spreads between short-term debt and long-term structured finance products such as asset-backed securities.
7. Collateralized debt obligations (CDOs) are a type of security backed by a pool of bonds, loans, and other assets. CDOs are assigned different risk classes, or tranches, with senior tranches considered the safest securities. Interest and principal payments are made in order of seniority, so that junior tranches offer higher interest rates and lower prices to compensate for the additional risk of default.

backed[8] Bear Stearns funds that collapsed in 2007, precipitating the credit crisis, were incorporated in the Caymans. Jersey and Guernsey, offshore financial centers in the Channel Islands, specialize in private equity. Many SIVs were created offshore, far from regulatory eyes.

We now know that hedge funds made their record profits from offshore bases by taking long-term gambles with short-term loans. The risky funds were often backed by onshore banks but kept off those institutions' books as they were repackaged and sold around the world. Regulators never took much notice: one, because lobbyists told them not to; two, because the funds were so complex that [financier] George Soros barely understood them; and three, because many of the deals were happening offshore.

Beneath regulatory radar, shadow bankers were able to scrap capital cushions, conceal illiquidity, and muddle debt accountability while depending on constant refinancing to survive. When the bubble burst and investors made a run for their money, panicked fund managers found it impossible to honor their debts, or even figure out how to price them as the markets crumbled. . . .

Last Laugh

This convoluted network of offshore escapades is what world leaders have vowed to bring under global regulatory watch in order to restore worldwide financial stability. To their credit, the crackdown on banking secrecy has already begun in a big way.

In February, secret Swiss bank accounts were blown open to permit an unprecedented Internal Revenue Service [IRS] probe. Europe's UBS bank has admitted to helping wealthy Americans evade what prosecutors believe to be $300 million a year in taxes.

8. Subprime mortgages are those to individuals with poor credit histories who would not be able to qualify for conventional mortgages. Higher interest rates are charged on subprime mortgages than conventional mortgages because of the increased risk of default for lenders.

Tax Haven Wage Economic Warfare

Stating that "tax havens are engaged in economic warfare against the United States, and honest, hardworking Americans", Sen. Carl Levin, D-Mich., Sen. Sheldon Whitehouse, D-RI, Sen. Claire McCaskill, D-Mo. and Sen. Bill Nelson, D-Fla., today [March 2, 2009,] introduced comprehensive legislation to stop offshore tax haven and tax shelter abuses. . . .

Offshore tax abuses cost the U.S. Treasury an estimated $100 billion each year in lost tax revenues, including $40–$70 billion from individuals and $30–$60 billion from corporations. Abusive domestic tax shelters cost tens of billions of dollars more.

Carl Levin, News Release, March 2, 2009.

Switzerland, the world's biggest tax haven where at least $2 trillion in offshore money is stashed, has long refused to recognize tax evasion as a crime. Every nation has the sovereign right to set its own tax code, which is why regulators have had such a hard time challenging offshore banking in the past. The dirty secret of tax havens, as President [Barack] Obama once noted, is that they're mostly legal.

Under U.S. law, tax avoidance (legal) only becomes tax evasion (illegal) in the absence of other, more credible perks. In other words, a company is free to establish foreign subsidiaries in search of financial expertise, global reach, convenience, etc., just so long as tax dodging does not appear to be the sole reason for relocation.

The IRS will tax individual American income wherever it's found, but finding it is often the key. To access account information in Switzerland, authorities had to have proof not merely of tax evasion but of fraud, which is what much white-knuckled investigation finally produced on UBS. In the wake of this success, and under threat of landing on the OECD's [Organization for Economic Development] new list of "uncooperative" tax havens, all of Europe's secrecy jurisdictions—Liechtenstein, Andorra, Austria, Luxembourg, and Switzerland—have signed information-sharing agreements.

Following the blood trail, congressional investigators descended on the Cayman Islands in March [2009] to tour the infamous Ugland House: one building supposedly home to 12,748 U.S. companies. The trip was an attempt to verify some of the implicit accusations made by a Government Accountability Office report in January [2009] which found that 83 of the United States' top 100 companies operate subsidiaries in tax havens.

Many of those, including Citigroup (which holds 90 subsidiaries in the Cayman Islands alone), Bank of America, and AIG, have received billions in taxpayer-funded bailouts. But the report failed to establish whether the subsidiaries were set up for the sole purpose of tax evasion.

Offshore Arguments

Politicians are already patting themselves on the back for their success in tackling tax crime. Everyone is making a big deal of the new tax information-exchange standard that all but three nations (Costa Rica, Malaysia, and the Philippines—the OECD's freshly minted blacklist) have agreed to implement in the wake of the G20 meeting.[9] What leaders aren't saying is that before it became a G20 talking point, tax information exchange was actually tax haven *fans'* favored reform measure.

The first thing most offshore officials claim when confronted with criticism is that their countries are not, indeed, tax havens. Since the OECD launched a tax policy campaign

9. The G-20 (or Group of 20) is a group of finance ministers (such as the U.S. secretary of the treasury) from twenty industrialized and emerging-market countries who meet to discuss economic issues.

in 1996, many of the offshore centers have been working to clean up their acts. A hoard of information-exchange agreements with onshore economies were signed even before Switzerland took the plunge. Geoff Cook, head of Jersey Finance, says Jersey's agreements with the United States, Germany, Sweden, and others have long outpaced what banks in Switzerland and Singapore traditionally maintained. "Our only fear in this is that people wouldn't look into the subject deep enough to draw those distinctions," Cook said.

But analysts say the agreements lack teeth. To request information from offshore, authorities must already have some evidence of misconduct. And the information-exchange standard still only covers illegal tax evasion, not legal tax avoidance. More importantly, what is already evident is that these agreements don't change much about the way offshore financial centers function. Offshore centers that agree to open up their books still have the luxury of setting their own regulatory standards and will continue to attract business based on their shadow banking credentials.

The G20 decided that shadow banking must be subjected to the same regulation as onshore commercial activity, which will also see more diligent oversight. Financial activity everywhere will be required to maintain better capital buffers, they said, monitored by a new Financial Stability Board; and excessive risk-taking will be rebuked. But the push for harmonized regulation across all financial centers revokes a degree of local liberty. Big ideas about state sovereignty and economic growth are at stake, which is probably what made [French president Nicolas] Sarkozy so nervous about taking his regulatory demands global.

"People come here for expertise and knowledge," argues head of Guernsey Finance Peter Niven, and he may have a point. Many in finance think it's wrong to put all the blame on private funds and offshore centers for a crisis of such complex origins. Havens say stripping away their financial freedoms is hypocritical and shortsighted. "It's really not about the Cayman Islands, it's about the U.S. tax gap—and we're the collateral damage," said one frustrated Cayman Island official, adding: "Everybody needs liquidity and everyone needs money. That's what we do."

Predictably, reform critics warn that responding to the global crisis with "too much" regulation will stifle economic growth, something they know world leaders are quite conscious of. "International Financial Centres such as Jersey play an important role as conduits in the flow of international capital around the world by providing liquidity in neighbouring (often onshore) financial centres, the very lubrication which markets now need," wrote Cook in a recent statement.

Overall, attempting to move beyond paltry information exchange to implementing real regulation of shadow banking across national jurisdictions promises to be extremely difficult.

Real Reform

Part of the solution starts at home. Offshore enthusiasts might be the first to point out that the Securities and Exchange Commission never had the remit to regulate onshore hedge funds because Congress didn't give it to them. Wall Street deregulation is often cited in Europe as the base rot in the system.

But demanding more regulation onshore won't do any good if you can't regulate in the same way offshore. A serious aspect of the tax haven problem is a kind of global regulatory arbitrage[10]: widespread onshore deregulation over the last 20 years came alongside an affinity for doing business offshore where even less regulation was possible, which in turn encour-

---

10. Arbitrage is a strategy in which investors profit from temporary discrepancies between the prices of the stocks comprising an index (stocks grouped together so their performance can be measured) and the price of a futures contract on that index. By buying either the stocks or the futures contract and selling the other, an investor can sometimes exploit market inefficiency for a profit.

aged tax haven-style policies in countries like Britain, the United States, Singapore, and Ireland, all fighting to draw finance back into their economies.

President Obama has long been a champion of both domestic and offshore financial reform, and a critic of the deregulation popular during the Bush years. But for global action to happen, Obama needs Europe's help (not to mention cooperation from Asia and the Middle East) and no one knows how deep [British prime minister] Gordon Brown's commitment runs. It is only very recently that Brown transformed himself from deregulation cheerleader as chancellor of the exchequer under [former UK prime minister] Tony Blair to global regulatory savior as Britain's new prime minister. . . .

Still, the regulatory tide is strong and rising; even global financial heavyweights may find it unwise or simply impossible to swim against it. For perhaps the first time since the end of World War II, the world appears open to the kind of global cooperation necessary to facilitate global integration in a socially responsible way.

But the tiny nations that have built empires around unfettered financial services will surely continue to fight for their place in the sun. Some may go the way of Darwinian selection. Declining tourism is already crippling economies across the Caribbean. But many more are optimistic about their ability to hang on. Guernsey is pursuing Chinese markets. Jersey claims business in private equity remains strong. Bermuda still has insurance and hopes to dabble in gambling. Many offshore say they welcome the coming reforms.

"We look forward to those challenges," said Michael Dunkley, leader of the United Bermuda Party, noting that Bermuda, a tiny island with a population of just 66,000 people, is not encumbered by big bureaucracy when it comes to getting things done. Whatever new regulations come up, he said: "Bermuda would be at the cutting edge of making sure it worked."

Accusations of capitalist evil aside, one can't help but admire their spirit.

| "Congress ... [has] even tried to scape-
goat the low-tax jurisdictions [offshore]
as somehow being responsible for the
global recession. This is nonsense."

Foreign Tax Havens Did Not Contribute to the Banking Crisis

Richard W. Rahn

From 2002 to 2008, Richard W. Rahn was the first non-Cayman member of the board of directors of the Cayman Islands Monetary Authority, which regulates the world's largest offshore financial center. He is also a senior fellow at the Cato Institute, a libertarian U.S. think tank; chairman of the Institute for Global Economic Growth; a weekly columnist for the Washington Times; *and a member of the editorial board of the* Cayman Financial Review.

In the following viewpoint Rahn criticizes efforts of U.S. legislators and the Barack Obama administration to impose taxes and regulations on the activities of foreign tax havens. He argues that these measures are not necessary because these jurisdictions already cooperate with the U.S. and other governments in pro-

viding tax exchange information. Rahn also dismisses charges that tax havens contributed to the financial crisis, contending that tax havens are merely transition points and provide a useful purpose in enabling the distribution of capital worldwide.

As you read, consider the following questions:

1. What are some of the benefits that the author cites of tax competition among nations?

2. Why does Rahn call the United States the world's largest tax haven for non-U.S. citizens?

3. What change in the tax code does the author recommend to solve the problem of foreign investment?

If the government suddenly said you would incur more onerous and expensive tax regulations and reporting requirements if you moved your business to a low-tax state such as Texas or Florida from a high-tax state such as New York or California, you would be justifiably outraged. Now substitute Switzerland and Bermuda for Texas and Florida, and France and Germany for New York and California, and you'll understand a new form of "tax protectionism" that is infecting Washington.

Several serious proposals are being floated in the nation's capital that would penalize Americans for investing in low-tax rather than high-tax jurisdictions. Proponents say the measures are needed to catch tax cheats—but ignore the fact that most of the low-tax jurisdictions such as the Cayman Islands, Switzerland, etc., already have tax information exchange (for cases of probable cause), or tax withholding, agreements with the U.S. and other countries such as the U.K. and France.

Nevertheless, Sens. Carl Levin (D., Mich.), Byron Dorgan (D., N.D.), and Max Baucus (D., Mont.), as well as officials of the Obama Treasury, want to make it more onerous and costly for American companies to do business around the world and for Americans to invest elsewhere. They would even make it more difficult for non-Americans to invest in the U.S.

Mr. Levin's bill is a hodgepodge of tax increases, more regulations and penalties on American taxpayers doing business in targeted low-tax jurisdictions. Mr. Dorgan's bill would prevent certain American companies that operate and are incorporated outside the U.S. from being treated as nondomestic corporations, thus denying them the right of tax deferral until their income is brought back to the U.S. Mr. Baucus, chairman of the Senate Finance Committee, is circulating a draft bill that, among other things, would extend the statute of limitations from three to six years for tax returns reporting international transactions. The Treasury Department is proposing expanded regulations on foreign financial institutions that bring needed investment funds into the U.S.

In addition to charges of tax evasion, some members of Congress—echoing European politicians including France's President Nicolas Sarkozy and British Prime Minister Gordon Brown—have even tried to scapegoat the low-tax jurisdictions as somehow being responsible for the global recession. They are demanding that the G-20[1] countries come up with action proposals against them at their meeting next month.

This is nonsense. The so-called tax havens are for the most part no more than way-stations to temporarily collect savings from around the world until they are invested in productive projects, such as building a new shopping center or semiconductor plant in the U.S. This enables a better allocation of world capital, leading to higher, not lower, global growth rates.

Indeed, to the extent tax competition between jurisdictions holds down the increase in the growth of governments, citizens of all countries experience more job opportunities and higher standards of living. And to the extent that busi-

1. The G-20 (or Group of Twenty) is a group of finance ministers (such as the U.S. secretary of the treasury) from twenty industrialized and emerging-market countries who meet to discuss economic issues.

Focus on Tax Havens Misplaced

There is no evidence that OFCs [offshore financial centers] played any role in the economic crisis and little evidence that fraud in conjunction with offshore accounts is any worse than fraud within onshore countries. After all, the $60+ billion fraud perpetuated by [Bernard] Madoff occurred squarely on U.S soil. There is, therefore, no reason for G-20 [a group of finance ministers from twenty industrialized and emerging market countries who meet to discuss economic issues] and OECD [Organization for Economic Co-operation and Development] membernations to punish OFCs disproportionately—other than to plunder their protected wealth to pay for massive bailouts and stimulus packages.

Simon Raftopoulos and Samuel Banks,
Cayman Islands Journal, *May 2009.*

nesses and individuals are discouraged by taxes or regulations from investing outside their own jurisdictions, they may simply choose to work and save less, period.

Those who demand increased taxes on global capital often rail against financial privacy and bank secrecy—forgetting they are necessary for civil society. It is true that not all people are saintly. But it is also true that not all governments are free from tyranny and corruption, and not all people are fully protected against criminal elements, even within their own governments. Without some jurisdictions in the world enforcing reasonable rights of financial privacy, those living in un-free and corrupt jurisdictions would have no place to protect their financial assets from kidnappers, extortionists, blackmailers and assorted government and nongovernment thugs.

It is a fool's errand to pass ever more laws against things that are already illegal, or to pass laws against people trying to protect themselves from rapacious and corrupt governments. Despite the hundreds of local, state and federal laws against financial fraud, and financial regulatory authorities like the SEC [Securities and Exchange Commission], Bernie Madoff was able to conduct the biggest ever Ponzi scheme for decades.

The chief tax writer in Congress, House Ways and Means Committee Chairman Charles Rangel, Treasury Secretary Timothy Geithner, and former Senate Majority Leader Tom Daschle apparently did not report all of their foreign-source income. Their actions tell us that either the tax law is too complex, or they thought the tax burden was excessive. Would their behavior and that of millions of others improve by making the tax law more complex and punitive?

U.S. companies are being forced to move elsewhere to remain internationally competitive because we have one of the world's highest corporate tax rates. And many economists, including Nobel Laureate Robert Lucas, have argued that the single best thing we can do to improve economic performance and job creation is to eliminate multiple taxes on capital gains, interest and dividends. Income is already taxed once, before it is invested, whether here or abroad; taxing it a second time as a capital gain only discourages investment and growth.

In fact, the U.S. does not tax most of the dividend, interest and capital gains' earnings of foreign investors in the U.S.—which means, ironically, that the U.S. is the world's largest "tax haven" for non-U.S. citizens, and that we benefit from hundreds of billions of dollars of needed capital invested here. If the U.S. did not treat foreign investors better than its own citizens (who are double-taxed on most capital income), most of the "tax avoidance" problems critics complain about would disappear.

The proposals by Messrs. Dorgan, Levin, Baucus and the Treasury will almost certainly have the unintended consequences of driving more U.S. businesses elsewhere, discouraging foreign investment in the U.S., and actually encouraging more U.S. investors to move their funds (either legally or illegally) not only out of the country, but to places in Asia or the Mideast that tend to be less cooperative with U.S. tax authorities than are the European and British low-tax jurisdictions.

The correct policy for the United States to follow is to reduce its corporate tax rate to make it internationally competitive, and to move toward a tax system that does not punish savings and productive investment so severely. We know from the experiences of many countries that reducing tax rates and simplifying the tax code improve both tax compliance and economic growth. Tax protectionism should be rejected because it is at least as destructive to economic growth and job creation as are tariffs on goods and services.

"[U.S. officials] end up either implicitly or overtly laying the blame [for the crisis] at the feet of China."

China Contributed to the Banking Crisis

Eswar Prasad

Eswar Prasad is a senior fellow in global economy and development and holds the New Century Chair in International Economics, at the Brookings Institution, an independent think tank. He is the Tolani Senior Professor of Trade Policy at Cornell University and a research associate at the National Bureau of Economic Research. Prasad was previously head of the Financial Studies Division and the China Division at the International Monetary Fund.

Prasad suggests in the following viewpoint that a fundamental cause of the financial meltdown was massive global trade imbalances, caused by excessive debt in the United States and excessive lending by China and other emerging market countries. He warns that solutions to the crisis need to be global, or these imbalances will continue.

Eswar Prasad, "The Global Financial Crisis: Getting Past the Blame Game," *The Brookings Institution*, January 28, 2009. Copyright © 2009 Brookings Institution. Reproduced by permission of voxeu.org.

As you read, consider the following questions:

1. What factors did the George W. Bush administration cite as creating the financial crisis, according to the author?

2. What are some of the worrisome ironies behind the crisis that Prasad feels may cause it to worsen unless a global solution is found?

3. What steps does the author recommend to address the financial problem?

Who's to blame for the worldwide financial crisis? The list of potential culprits for the meltdown of the US financial system is long and the rogues' gallery will no doubt expand a great deal before the economy is out of the woods. But a worldwide crisis calls for a global villain. And there is indeed one at hand—global macroeconomic imbalances, characterised by large current account deficits in the US and a few other advanced industrial countries, with these deficits financed by excess savings in China and many other emerging market economies.

Did Trade Imbalances Cause the Crisis?

That depends on whom you ask. Whatever the right answer, however, we must guard against the risk that these imbalances could actually worsen during the global recovery—whenever that comes—and set the stage for the global economy to stumble again in the future.

The view from the US, which has been at the epicentre of the crisis, is interesting. In its waning days, the [George W.] Bush White House issued a statement that in part reads "... the President highlighted a factor that economists agree on: that the most significant factor leading to the housing crisis was cheap money flowing into the US from the rest of the world, so that there was no natural restraint on flush lenders

China Laid Foundation for Crisis

Over the past decade, China and other emerging markets accumulated foreign currency reserves to insure against the economic and political vagaries of financial globalisation. They were wise to do so. Countries with larger reserves are weathering the storm relatively better than those who have bought less insurance.

Although purchasing insurance policy might have been sensible from the perspective of each country, collectively these currency interventions prepared the ground for the global crisis. Emerging markets, most notably China, helped to create the macroeconomic backdrop for the current financial crisis by subsidising interest rates and consumption in the US.

Moritz Schularick,
Financial Times *blog,*
August 5, 2009. www.ft.com.

to push loans on Americans in risky ways. This flow of funds into the US was unprecedented. And because it was unprecedented, the conditions it created presented unprecedented questions for policymakers." In other words, it's all the foreigners' fault.

This builds on [chairman of the Federal Reserve Board Ben] Bernanke's saving glut hypothesis, and officials in the new [Obama] administration seem to have picked up the theme. These statements invariably end up either implicitly or overtly laying the blame at the feet of China for its currency management policies that have created a current account surplus that could amount to about $350 billion, or about 9% of GDP [gross domestic product], in 2008.

Global Imbalances and US Financial Problems

There is no doubt that global imbalances allowed problems in the US financial system to fester. Excess savings in Asian and other emerging markets and the bloated revenues of oil-exporting countries were recycled into the US financial markets. The resulting low interest rates in the US created incentives for financial shenanigans in the US and blocked self-correcting mechanisms such as rising interest rates due to higher government borrowing. What could have been a bubble that would sooner or later have popped instead turned into a blimp that soared heavenward before crashing back to earth.

The Chinese, for their part, have reacted with scorn to the notion that anyone but the US bears central blame for the crisis. In any event, whether or not one regards global imbalances as the root cause of the crisis, the underlying policies that generated those imbalances were clearly not in the long-term interests of the countries concerned.

US fiscal profligacy and a financial system that encouraged the consumption binge helped bring on the financial instability. For its part, China has done itself no favours with a currency regime that has tied its hands on macroeconomic policy, kept its economy dependent on exports (most of which go the US and the EU [European Union]), and hindered a much-needed rebalancing of growth towards private consumption. In a cruel irony, the thriftiness of the Chinese has come back to haunt them with the collapse in the demand for their exports.

Indeed, there is an even richer set of ironies in the way the crisis has played out.

- First, the global macro imbalances are not unravelling in the way that many economists had expected (present company included). Rather than experiencing a decline in the value of the dollar, the US current account deficit may apparently adjust with just a massive contraction in private consumption.

- Second, the epicentre of the crisis has become the safe haven, with the flight to quality around the world turning into a flight to US treasury bonds.

- Third, and most worryingly, the rest of the world still seems to be counting on the US as a demander of last resort.

- Fourth, all signs are that the global crisis may lead to emerging markets rethinking old notions of reserve adequacy and consider building up even larger stocks of reserves.

In short, as the world economy pulls out of the crisis, the imbalances that created much of the problem could intensify rather than dissipate. This is why the solutions need to be global as well. Moreover, while much has been said about how to redesign financial regulation, this has to be supported by a clear focus on macroeconomic policies.

Some of the necessary steps are as follows.

Additional macroeconomic stimulus measures are clearly going to be needed in all of the major economies. These should be coordinated in order to prevent the stimulus in any one country from seeping out and reducing the overall bang for the buck. Moreover, coordination would also bolster business and consumer confidence that governments are serious about stimulating their economies with all tools available and enlightened enough to do this in a cooperative manner.

The major world economies need to map out and forcefully communicate their strategies to solve their domestic problems. For instance, the U.S. needs clear plans to bring its public finances under control over a reasonable horizon after the recovery gets going and to retool its financial regulatory mechanisms. The Chinese need to have an effective strategy to rebalance their economy towards private consumption and away from investment and exports. This will require greater social spending and a more flexible exchange rate.

A revamp of global governance is essential. The IMF [International Monetary Fund] (or an equivalent institution) needs to be given the teeth to call not just emerging markets but also the rich industrial economies to the woodshed when they run policies that might be in their apparent short-term self-interest but against the collective long-term interests of the world economy. It also needs to have enough resources and sufficient legitimacy among emerging markets that they can count on it as an insurer, and thereby save themselves the trouble and costs of self-insuring by building up large stocks of reserves.

While financial regulatory reform is needed, reform of the international arrangements for macroeconomic policy surveillance and the international financial architecture are equally urgent priorities. Otherwise, we will be back where we started, with a perfectly good crisis gone to waste.

"*China and other emerging economies were obviously not the leading powers in the global economy and therefore not able to cause the current crisis.*"

China Did Not Cause the Banking Crisis

Huang Xin

Huang Xin reports for the Xinhua News Agency, an official Chinese news agency.

In the following viewpoint, the author contends that many U.S. government officials are attempting to blame China for the global financial crisis. The author rebuts these claims, laying the blame instead on U.S. monetary policy, which kept interest rates too low and encouraged reckless spending.

As you read, consider the following questions:

1. According to the author, when did the U.S. dollar become the currency most used in international transactions?

2. Huang Xin states that losses in the U.S. stock market were less than in which other countries?

3. What does the author cite as the root cause of the financial crisis?

Plagued by the financial crisis that originated in the United States, the world economy has been thrown into chaos. While countries are battling the crisis, outgoing U.S. Treasury Secretary Henry Paulson has been playing a blame game.

Paulson said a failure to address the rise of emerging markets and resulting imbalances was partly to blame for the global financial crisis. The current U.S. Federal Reserve Chairman, Ben Bernanke, is also part of the game. He sees savings from countries like China as a cause of the property bubble in the United States.

Their remarks made headlines but cannot change the facts. It is widely accepted that the U.S. low interest rate policy, which encouraged excessive spending and caused the subprime crisis,[1] was at the root of the problem.

The Fed [Federal Reserve] used this policy to save the country's economy from a contraction in the 1990s, when China and other emerging economies had no large trade surplus or savings.

Apparently, Paulson has mixed up cause and effect by suggesting that emerging economies pushed down U.S. interest rates.

Since former President Richard Nixon took the United States off the gold standard in 1971, the U.S. dollar has been the currency most used in international transactions.

The United States remains the world's largest economy and the status of the dollar has not changed radically. China and other emerging economies were obviously not the leading powers in the global economy and therefore not able to cause the current crisis.

---

1. The subprime mortgage crisis is the financial crisis caused by a dramatic rise in mortgage defaults and foreclosures in the United States, with major adverse consequences for banks and financial markets around the globe.

Westerners to Blame for Crisis

[British prime minister] Gordon Brown's efforts to smooth a path to international agreement at [the March 2009 G20 (Group of Twenty developed and emerging nations)] summit in London hit a bump in Brazil when he was told that the financial crisis was the fault of the "white and blue-eyed".

President Lula da Silva of Brazil warned that there would be spicy discussions and "tough confrontation" [at the summit] as world leaders faced up to who should pay the costs of the banking crisis.

Francis Elliott, Times *(London), March 27, 2009.*

As the ancient Chinese sage Confucius said: "On seeing a man without virtue, examine yourself to be sure you do not have the same defects."

Even some American scholars agreed that internal problems, including over-spending, rampant use of financial derivatives[2] and lack of market supervision resulted in a low savings rate and huge U.S. trade deficits.

The U.S.-borne crisis has hurt stock markets around the world. China's Shanghai Composite Index lost 65.4 percent last year [2008], the seventh-largest decline among world markets. Iceland's OMX Index had the biggest loss of 94.4 percent.

Amazingly, there were no U.S. stock indices on the list of the top 20 losers. Although New York's three stock indices fell

---

2. A derivative is a financial instrument whose value is derived from an underlying asset, index, event, value, or condition. The derivative itself is merely a contract to exchange cash or assets over time based on fluctuations in the underlying assets. Most derivatives are characterized by high leverage, or debt.

to the levels they were at 10 years ago, the drops were much smaller than markets elsewhere.

Analysts say U.S. investment institutions sell off overseas assets when facing a credit crunch at home, which results in disastrous withdrawals of foreign capital from some emerging markets. This was why the woes of the United States have inflicted pain on the world economy at large.

If we compare the U.S. economy to a car, emerging markets have somehow served as windshields amid the battering of the financial storm. Can we blame the windshields for the failure of a car?

Imbalances in global trade and investment did have a role in the crisis but were not at the root of the problem. Loose supervision that helped pump excessive dollars into circulation was the root cause.

When a morally upright person is mired in difficulties, he or she will engage in introspection rather than shift responsibility. China has moved to cope with the problem with a stream of measures and so have other large world economies.

It is not time to play a blame game. Regulators in the United States might not want to miss the chance that they failed to seize before the crisis, when property companies, investment banks and insurance companies juggled various financial products and Wall Street "elites" snatched tens of millions out of the bubble.

Periodical Bibliography

The following articles have been selected to supplement the diverse views presented in this chapter.

Jenny Booth — "China and Russia Blame U.S. for Financial Crisis," *Times* (London), January 29, 2009.

Paul Cavey — "Now China Has a Credit Boom," *Wall Street Journal*, July 30, 2009.

David M. Dickson — "China's Buying Binge Focused on Mae, Mac; Holds $1.1 Trillion in U.S. Debt," *Washington Times*, May 7, 2009.

Ding Yifan — "Crisis Should Make U.S. Do Some Soul-Searching," *China Daily*, February 2, 2009.

James Fallows — "Be Nice to the Countries That Lend You Money," *Atlantic Monthly*, December 2008.

Marcus Gee — "Chinese Thriftiness No Saving Grace," *Globe and Mail* (Toronto), April 9, 2009.

Li Xiaokun and Zhang Haizhou — "Financial Crisis 'Not China's Fault,'" *China Daily*, January 21, 2009.

Michael Mandel — "A Simple Guide to the Banking Crisis," *Business Week*, March 12, 2009.

Thomas Omestad — "Chinese Blame U.S. Policies for Financial Crisis During Economic Talks," *U.S. News & World Report*, December 4, 2008.

Alan Rappeport — "Foreign Money Continues to Pour into U.S.," *Financial Times*, February 17, 2009.

Moritz Schularick — "How China Helped Create the Macroeconomic Backdrop for Financial Crisis," *Financial Times*, February 24, 2009.

Glossary

Amortization is the allocation of a lump sum amount to different time periods, particularly for loans, including related interest or other finance charges.

Arbitrage is a strategy in which investors profit from temporary discrepancies between the prices of the stocks comprising an index (stocks grouped together so their performance can be measured) and the price of a futures contract on that index. By buying either the stocks or the futures contract and selling the other, an investor can sometimes exploit market inefficiency for a profit.

Collateralized debt obligations (CDOs) are a type of security backed by a pool of bonds, loans, and other assets. CDOs are assigned different risk classes, or tranches, with senior tranches considered the safest securities. Interest and principal payments are made in order of seniority, so that junior tranches offer higher interest rates and lower prices to compensate for the additional risk of default.

Conduits are government or private organizations that assemble mortgages and other loans into a large pool and issue securities in the name of the conduit to investors.

A credit default swap (CDS) is a transaction where the buyer of a bond or loan makes payments to the seller, who guarantees the creditworthiness of the product. The buyer receives a payment from the seller if the product goes into default.

Deregulation is the removal or easing of government rules and regulations in the economic system.

A derivative is a financial instrument whose value is derived from an underlying asset, index, event, value, or condition. The derivative itself is merely a contract to exchange cash or assets over time based on fluctuations in the underlying assets. Most derivatives are characterized by high leverage, or debt.

Employee stock options are employee benefits that include the opportunity to purchase stock under favorable terms, or to have stock awarded.

An equity is ownership interest in a corporation in the form of common or preferred stock.

An equity fund is a mutual fund that invests primarily in stocks, usually common stocks.

In the futures industry, investors contract to buy or sell a specified commodity of standardized quality at a certain date in the future, at a market-determined price. The contracts are traded on a futures exchange.

The G-20 (or Group of Twenty) is a group of finance ministers (such as the U.S. secretary of the treasury) from twenty industrialized and emerging-market countries who meet to discuss economic issues.

A golden parachute is a clause in an employment agreement guaranteeing an executive lucrative severance benefits if a company is sold or management control otherwise changes hands.

The Group of Thirty, established in 1978, is a private, non-profit, international body composed of very senior representatives of the private and public sectors and academia.

GSEs are government-sponsored enterprises, a group of financial institutions created by the U.S. Congress; e.g., Fannie Mae.

A hedge fund is a pooled private investment fund that seeks to maximize returns with strategies that include unconventional investments and investments that cannot quickly be converted to cash, such as real estate.

An index is a group of stocks whose performance is measured as a group.

An interest rate swap is a financial transaction often used by hedge funds in which one party exchanges a stream of interest payments for the other party's stream of cash flows.

A junk bond is a bond rated BB or lower because it has a high risk of default.

Junk mortgages are those granted to people who have low credit scores and are at risk of defaulting on their mortgages.

Laissez-faire capitalism is a political philosophy promoting limited or no government regulation of business matters.

Leverage is the use of debt to grow an investment.

Liquidity is the ability of an asset to be quickly converted to cash without affecting the asset's price.

The M2 money supply consists of currency outside the U.S. Treasury, Federal Reserve Banks, and depository institution vaults—traveler's checks of nonbank issuers, demand deposits, other checkable deposits, and time deposits at commercial banks, excluding large CDs (certificates of deposit).

A Mortgage-backed security (MBS) is a debt obligation to the cash flows from a pool of mortgage loans, commonly on residential property. These securities are created when a financial institution buys mortgages from a primary lender, sells them in a bundle to investors, and uses the monthly mortgage payments to pay the investors.

Nationalization is taking an enterprise into public ownership by a national government.

A negative amortization loan is one where the payment by the borrower is less than the interest due and the difference is added to the loan balance. Thus, over time, the debt increases rather than is reduced, as in conventional mortgages.

A NINJA loan is a subprime loan issued to a buyer with no income, no job, and no assets.

Nonprime mortgages are those given to individuals with a FICO (Fair Isaac Corporation), or credit, score under 620.

An oligarchy is a system where power resides with a small, elite group of inside individuals and institutions who act together to control the system.

An Option ARM is an adjustable rate mortgage that typically offers four choices for repayment: a fully amortizing (eliminating by paying off over a period of time) 30-year payment, in which both principal and interest are paid on a 30-year schedule; a fully amortizing 15-year payment, in which both principal and interest are paid on a 15-year schedule; an interest-only payment, in which only the interest portion of the mortgage is paid, and not the principal; and a minimum payment, a widely-picked option in which the payment is set for 12 months at a low introductory interest rate. After that, payment changes are made annually and a payment cap limits how much it can increase or decrease each year.

Private equity companies invest in companies that are not publicly traded on a stock exchange. Investments in private equity typically involve either the acquisition of an operating company or the investment of capital into an operating company.

A procyclical system is one in which there is a direct, positive correlation between an event and the state of the economy; that is, any quantity that tends to increase when the overall economy is growing is classified as procyclical.

The Sarbanes-Oxley Act was enacted following a number of corporate and accounting scandals, and set more rigorous accounting standards for publicly traded companies.

A security is an investment instrument issued by a corporation, government, or other organization (excluding insurance policies and fixed annuities) that represents financial value. Securities can be debt (such as banknotes or bonds), equity (such as stocks), or derivatives (such as futures, options, or swaps).

Securitization is the process of aggregating similar types of investments, typically loans or mortgages, into a common pool, then selling that pool of investments.

The shadow banking system consists of nonbank financial institutions, such as hedge funds, that act as intermediaries between investors and borrowers.

Structured investment vehicles (SIVs) are pools of investment assets that attempt to profit from credit spreads between short-term debt and long-term structured finance products such as asset-backed securities (ABS).

The subprime mortgage crisis is the financial crisis caused by a dramatic rise in mortgage defaults and foreclosures in the United States, with major adverse consequences for banks and financial markets around the globe.

Subprime mortgages are those to individuals with poor credit histories and ratings (often below 600) who would not be able to qualify for conventional mortgages. Higher interest rates are charged on subprime mortgages than on conventional mortgages because of the increased risk of default for lenders.

Toxic assets are those assets whose value has dropped so sharply that they are no longer saleable.

A tranche is one of a number of related securities offered as part of the same transaction. Each tranche in the transaction is assigned a different risk class.

For Further Discussion

Chapter 1

1. In assessing blame for the banking crisis, Simon Johnson faults Wall Street, while Lawrence H. White blames Washington, D.C. Both agree that government policies contributed to the crisis; however, Johnson argues that the government was manipulated by the banking industry. Both cite facts and examples to support their claims. Citing the viewpoints, which evidence do you find more compelling? Why?

2. Nouriel Roubini argues that the lack of regulation under the George W. Bush administration caused the banking crisis, while James L. Gattuso refutes this view, contending that financial services were not deregulated under this administration. Roubini was a senior advisor to the Bill Clinton administration and Gattuso works for The Heritage Foundation, a conservative think tank. Do you think the authors' political affiliations help shape their arguments? How?

Chapter 2

1. Christina Romer claims that the actions being taken by the Barack Obama administration will restore the U.S. economy to strength, while Sandy B. Lewis and William D. Cohan disagree, saying the administration's efforts do not address what is fundamentally wrong with the banking system. Citing from the viewpoints, which of these conflicting arguments do you find more compelling, and why?

2. Both Barack Obama and Daniel Mitchell admit that the bailouts are rewarding banks for bad decisions that they

made. Mitchell gives this as a reason why the bailouts are bad for the economy, since they could encourage further risky behavior on the part of banks. Obama says the bailouts are necessary to get money flowing again and bring a quicker end to the banking crisis. do you think the bailout of banks was a good thing? Explain, citing evidence from the viewpoints.

3. Ben S. Bernanke and Thomas M. Hoenig disagree on the "too big to fail" question. Bernanke argues that the failure of a large bank would have a devastating effect on the financial system, while Hoenig disputes this and cites examples from recent history where large banks failed without injuring the economy. Do you think some institutions are too big to let fail? Explain your answer, citing from the viewpoints.

Chapter 3

1. Christopher J. Dodd and Steven Pearlstein share a reluctance to grant the Federal Reserve greater authority in regulating the activities of big banks. What are some of the problems that each sees with giving the Federal Reserve greater power?

2. Gene Sperling argues that executive compensation packages in banking need to be addressed to prevent the risky behavior that occurs when executives are rewarded for short-term results. Floyd Norris contends that regulating executive compensation will not solve problems in the financial system, because executive compensation did not cause the crisis. What are some of the assumptions about executive compensation that both authors share? What are some of the differences?

Chapter 4

1. Rachel Keeler contends that foreign tax havens contributed to the banking crisis, since many of the riskiest in-

vestments were placed offshore where there were few regulations. Richard W. Rahn argues that tax havens are merely transition points for international commerce and they in no way contributed to the crisis. What evidence does each author offer to support his argument? Does the type of evidence each provides make one argument more or less persuasive for you? Explain, citing from the viewpoints.

2. Eswar Prasad and the Xinhua News Agency disagree on the role that Chinese investment in the United States played in the banking crisis. Prasad cites it as a fundamental cause of the crisis, while the Xinhua News Agency says it was U.S. monetary policy, not Chinese investment, that caused the crisis. Citing from the viewpoints, which of these conflicting arguments do you find more persuasive? Or, is it possible that both arguments are valid? Explain your answer.

Organizations to Contact

The editors have compiled the following list of organizations concerned with all the issues debated in this book. The descriptions are derived from materials provided by the organizations. All have publications or information available for interested readers. The names, addresses, phone and fax numbers, and e-mail and Internet addresses may change. Be aware that many organizations take several weeks or longer to respond to inquiries, so allow as much time as possible.

American Economic Association (AEA)
2014 Broadway, Suite 305, Nashville, TN   37203
(615) 322-2595 • fax: (615) 343-7590
e-mail: aeainfo@vanderbilt.edu
Web site: www.americaneconomicassociation.org

The American Economic Association is a scholarly organization composed of economists from academic, business, government, and other professional institutions. The purposes of the association are to encourage economic research, issue publications on economic subjects, and promote the freedom of economic discussion. The AEA publishes the *American Economic Review*, the *Journal of Economic Literature*, the *Journal of Economic Perspectives*, and the *American Economic Journal*. It also makes journal articles and conference papers available to the general public on its Web site.

Bretton Woods Committee (BWC)
1990 M St. NW, Suite 450, Washington, DC   20036
(202) 331-1616 • fax: (202) 785-9423
e-mail: info@brettonwoods.org
Web site: www.brettonwoods.org

The BWC is a bipartisan group dedicated to increasing public understanding of international financial and development issues and the role of the World Bank, International Monetary

Fund, and World Trade Organization. Members include industry and financial leaders, economists, university leaders, and former government officials. On its Web site, the BWC publishes the quarterly *BWC Newsletter* as well as various reports, including "The United States and the WTO: Benefits of the Multilateral Trade System."

Brookings Institution

1775 Massachusetts Ave. NW, Washington, DC   20036
(202) 797-6000 • fax: (202) 797-6004
e-mail: communications@brookings.edu
Web site: www.brookings.edu

The Brookings Institution is a nonpartisan, nonprofit public policy think tank. Its mission is to conduct independent research and to provide innovative and practical recommendations that advance three broad goals. Those goals are to strengthen US democracy; foster the economic and social welfare, security and opportunity of all Americans; and secure a more open, safe, prosperous, and cooperative international system. The Economic Studies Program monitors the global economy and seeks answers to economic policy issues in the United States and worldwide. The Brookings Institution Press publishes books, journals, and policy papers and makes newsletters, research, commentary, and podcasts available to the general public on its Web site.

Cato Institute

1000 Massachusetts Ave. NW, Washington, DC   20001-5403
(202) 842-0200 • fax: (202) 842-3490
e-mail: cato@cato.org
Web site: www.cato.org

The Cato Institute is a libertarian public policy research foundation dedicated to promoting the limited role of government and protecting individual liberties. One of the areas of research for the Cato Institute is finance, banking, and monetary policy. The institute publishes books, journals including the *Cato Journal* and the *Cato Policy Report*, opinion, commentary, testimony, and speeches. Most of these are available to the general public on the institute's Web site.

Center for Economic and Policy Research (CEPR)
1611 Connecticut Ave. NW, Suite 400, Washington, DC   20009
(202) 293-5380 • fax: (202) 588-1356
e-mail: cepr@cepr.net
Web site: www.cepr.net

The CEPR is a progressive economic policy think tank that does research on social security, the U.S. housing bubble, developing-country economies, and gaps in the social policy fabric of the U.S. economy. The mission of the CEPR is to promote democratic debate on economic and social issues. CEPR conducts both professional research and public education. The organization provides reports and briefing papers to the general public on its Web site and has published extensively on the banking crisis.

The Heritage Foundation
214 Massachusetts Ave. NE, Washington, DC   20002
(202) 546-4400 • fax: (202) 546-0904
e-mail: info@heritage.org
Web site: www.heritage.com

The Heritage Foundation is a conservative think tank that supports and promotes the principles of free enterprise and limited government. Its many publications includes the *Backgrounder* series. One of the institute's areas of research is free enterprise and free markets, and it provides research, commentary, blogs, and charts on this topic on its Web site for the general public.

Hudson Institute
1015 Fifteenth St. NW, 6th Floor, Washington, DC   20005
(202) 974-2400 • fax: (202) 974-2410
e-mail: info@hudson.org
Web site: www.hudson.org

The Hudson Institute is a conservative think tank engaged in research and analysis to promote global security, prosperity, and freedom and to advise global leaders in government and business. The future-oriented institute undertakes interdisciplinary and collaborative studies in defense, international relations, economics, culture, science, technology, and law. Articles, papers, an electronic newsletter, reports, speeches, testimony, and white papers are available to the general public from the institute's Web site.

Independent Community Bankers of America (ICBA)

1615 L St. NW, Suite 900, Washington, DC   20036
(202) 659-8111 • fax: (202) 659-3604
e-mail: info@icba.org
Web site: www.icba.org

The Independent Community Bankers of America represents five thousand community banks of all sizes and charter types throughout the United States and is dedicated exclusively to representing the interests of the community banking industry and the communities and customers they serve.

The ICBA supports fair competition for financial institutions, supports maintaining the separation of banking and commerce, believes in a balanced financial system and opposes the concentration of economic and financial services resources. It provides electronic magazines and newsletters, titled *Independent Bankers Magazine, ICBA NewsWatch Today*, and *ICBA Washington Report* on its Web site.

International Monetary Fund (IMF)

700 Nineteenth St. NW, Washington, DC   20431
(202) 623-7000 • fax: (202) 623-4661
e-mail: publicaffairs@imf.org
Web site: www.imf.org

The IMF is an international organization of 184 member countries. It was established to promote international monetary cooperation, exchange stability, and orderly exchange arrangements. IMF seeks to foster economic growth and high levels of employment and provides temporary financial assistance to countries. It publishes the quarterly *Finance & Development* as well as reports on its activities, including the quarterly "Global Financial Stability Report," recent issues of which are available on its Web site along with data on IMF finances and individual country reports.

Mortgage Bankers Association (MBA)

1331 L St. NW, Washington, DC   20005
(202) 557-2700
e-mail: membership@mortgagebankers.org
Web site: www.mortgagebankers.org

The Mortgage Bankers Association is the national association representing the real estate finance industry. The mission of the MBA is to ensure the continued strength of the nation's residential and commercial real estate markets, expand home-ownership, extend access to affordable housing to all Americans, and support financial literacy efforts. The association provides research, commentaries, forecasts, statistics, and outlooks on its Web site for the general public, as well as making additional information available to members.

National Association of Affordable Housing Lenders (NAAHL)

1667 K St. NW, Suite 210, Washington, DC   20006
(202) 293-9850 • fax: (202) 293-9852
e-mail: info@naahl.org
Web site: www.naahl.org

The National Association of Affordable Housing Lenders consists of two hundred organizations committed to increasing private lending and investing in low- and moderate-income communities. Members include banks, thrifts, insurance companies, community development corporations, mortgage companies, loan consortia, financial intermediaries, pension funds, foundations, local and national nonprofits, and public agencies. The NAAHL publishes reports, audio forums, and resource books.

National Bankers Association (NBA)
1513 P St. NW, Washington, DC   20005
(202) 588-5432
e-mail: nahart@nationalbankers.org
Web site: www.nationalbankers.org

The National Bankers Association is a trade association for minority and women-owned banks (MWOBs). Members include banks owned by African Americans, Native Americans, East Indians, Hispanic Americans, Asian Americans, and women. MWOBs, with few exceptions, serve distressed communities plagued by many social and economic problems. Members of the NBA are institutions who are committed to providing employment opportunities, entrepreneurial capital, and economic revitalization in neighborhoods that often have little or no access to alternative financial services.

Peter G. Peterson Institute for International Economics
1750 Massachusetts Ave. NW, Washington, DC   20036
(202) 328-9000 • fax: (202) 650-3225
Web site: www.iie.com

The Peter G. Peterson Institute for International Economics is a private nonprofit, nonpartisan research institution devoted to the study of international economic policy. Its agenda emphasizes global macroeconomic topics, international money and finance, trade and related social issues, energy and the environment, investment, and domestic adjustment policies. Current priorities of the institute are the global financial and economic crisis, globalization, international trade imbalances and currency relationships, the creation of an international regime to address global warming (especially its trade dimension), the competitiveness of the United States and other major countries, reform of the international economic and financial architecture, sovereign wealth funds, and trade negotiations at the multilateral, regional, and bilateral levels. The institute publishes books and papers on economic issues and makes policy briefs, working papers, speeches, testimony, and commentary available to the general public on its Web site.

World Bank
1818 H St. NW, Washington, DC   20433
(202) 477-1234 • fax: (202) 577-0565
e-mail: wbannualreport@worldbank.org
Web site: www.worldbank.org

The World Bank was established by the United Nations to reduce poverty and improve the standard of living of poor
people around the world. It promotes sustainable growth and
investments in developing countries through loans, technical
assistance, and policy guidance. The bank makes documents
and reports available to the public on its Web site, including a
policy paper on the financial crisis, "What the World Bank Is
Doing."

Bibliography of Books

Viral Acharya and Matthew Richardson, eds.
Restoring Financial Stability: How to Repair a Failed System. Hoboken, NJ: John Wiley, 2009.

Keith Ambachtsheer, David Beatty, and Lawrence Booth
The Financial Crisis and Rescue: What Went Wrong? Why? What Lessons Can Be Learned? Toronto: University of Toronto Press, 2008.

William K. Black
The Best Way to Rob a Bank Is to Own One: How Corporate Executives and Politicians Looted the S&L Industry. Austin: University of Texas Press, 2005.

Dimitris N. Chorafas
Financial Boom and Gloom: The Credit and Banking Crisis of 2007–2009 and Beyond. New York: Palgrave Macmillan, 2009.

Jochen Felsenheimer and Philip Gisdakis
Credit Crises: From Tainted Loans to a Global Economic Meltdown. Weinheim, Germany: Wiley-VCH, 2008.

John Bellamy Foster and Fred Magdoff
The Great Financial Crisis: Causes and Consequences. New York: Monthly Review Press, 2009.

Paul Krugman
The Return of Depression Economics and the Crisis of 2008. New York: Norton, 2008.

Paul Mason
Meltdown: The End of the Age of Greed. New York: Verso, 2009.

Lawrence G. McDonald with Patrick Robinson *A Colossal Failure of Common Sense: The Inside Story of the Collapse of Lehman Brothers.* New York: Crown Business, 2009.

Adam Michaelson *The Foreclosure of America: The Inside Story of the Rise and Fall of Countrywide Home Loans, the Mortgage Crisis, and the Default of the American Dream.* New York: Berkley Books, 2009.

Charles R. Morris *The Trillion Dollar Meltdown.* New York: Public Affairs, 2008.

Paul Muolo *Chain of Blame: How Wall Street Caused the Mortgage Banking and Credit Crisis.* Hoboken, NJ: John Wiley, 2008.

Johan Norberg *Financial Fiasco: How America's Infatuation with Home Ownership and Easy Money Created the Financial Crisis.* Washington, DC: Cato Institute, 2009.

Frank Partnoy *Infectious Greed: How Deceit and Risk Corrupted the Financial Markets.* New York: Public Affairs, 2009.

Kevin Phillips *Bad Money: Reckless Finance, Failed Politics, and the Global Crisis of American Capitalism.* New York: Viking, 2009.

Nomi Prins   *It Takes a Pillage: Behind the Bailouts, Bonuses, and Backroom Deals from Washington to Wall Street.* Hoboken, NJ: John Wiley, 2009.

Colin Read   *Global Financial Meltdown: How We Can Avoid the Next Economic Crisis.* New York: Palgrave Macmillan, 2009.

Herman M. Schwartz   *Subprime Nation: American Power, Global Capital, and the Housing Bubble.* Ithaca, NY: Cornell University Press, 2009.

Peter Schweizer   *Architects of Ruin: How a Generation of Liberal Activists, Politicians, and Bankers Brought the Global Economy to Its Knees.* New York: HarperCollins, 2009.

Robert J. Shiller   *The Subprime Solution: How Today's Global Financial Crisis Happened, and What to Do About It.* Princeton, NJ: Princeton University Press, 2008.

Andrew Ross Sorkin   *Too Big to Fail: The Inside Story of How Wall Street and Washington Fought to Save the Financial System from Crisis—and Lost.* New York: Viking, 2009.

George Soros   *The New Paradigm for Financial Markets: The Credit Crisis of 2008 and What It Means.* New York: Public Affairs, 2008.

John B. Taylor

Getting Off Track: How Government Actions and Intervention Caused, Prolonged, and Worsened the Financial Crisis. Stanford, CA: Hoover Institution Press, 2009.

Katrina Vanden Heuvel et al.

Meltdown: How Greed and Corruption Shattered Our Financial System and How We Can Recover. New York: Nation Books, 2009.

David Wessel

In Fed We Trust: Ben Bernanke's War on the Great Panic. New York: Crown Business, 2009.

Mark M. Zandi

Financial Shock: A 360° Look at the Subprime Mortgage Implosion, and How to Avoid the Next Financial Crisis. Upper Saddle River, NJ: Financial Times Press, 2009.

Index

A

Accountability, 62, 141, 211, 213
ACORN (Association of Community Organization for Reform Now), 46
Acquisitions and mergers
  Bank of America acquisition of Merril Lynch & Co., 20, 39, 62, 167
  risk management, 16
  too-big-to-fail banks and, 166
Adjustable rate mortgages (ARMs)
  Community Reinvestment Act and, 15
  effects of, 18–19
  Federal Reserve interest rates and, 42–43
  "special affordable" loans, 47
  See also Mortgage, Subprime mortgages
Affordable housing, 46, 47
African Americans, 54, 56
Alternative Mortgage Transaction Parity Act of 1982, 15
American Economic Review (magazine), 122
American International Group (AIG)
  bailout, 20, 35, 169
  CEO, 104
  collapse, 16, 41
  Federal Reserve and, 117
  government regulation and, 162, 173
  mortgage-backed security investment insurance, 108
American Prospect (magazine), 168

Andorra, 213
Arbitrage, 68, 68n1, 157, 157n1, 215, 215n10
Argentina, 26
Asia, 68
Association of Community Organization for Reform Now (ACORN), 46
Atlantic Magazine, 165
Austria, 213

B

Bahamas, 210, 216
Bailout Nation (Ritholtz), 22
Bailouts
  AIG, 20, 35, 169
  banking industry, 20, 32, 35, 84, 169
  criticism of, 100–101, 115–121
  deregulation and, 61
  hedge funds, 102
  negative economic effect, 117–119
  Obama endorsement, 106–114
  socialized losses, 119
  taxpayer response, 201
  Wall Street Journal and, 52
  wasted money, 144, 147
Baily, Martin Neil, 89, 156
Bair, Sheila C., 124, 165, 169, 175
Baker, Dean, 170
Balloon mortgages, 15
Banana republics, 26–28
Bank Accountability and Risk Assessment Act of 2009, 181

Bank of America
 bailout, 32
 BlackRock ownership, 103
 CEO, 104, 167
 Continental Bank purchase by,
  150
 foreign tax havens, 213
 Merrill Lynch acquisition, 20,
  39, 62, 167
Bank of England, 70
Banking industry
 bailout, 20, 32, 35
 bankruptcies, 38
 commercial banks as investment banks, 16, 23, 29
 debt-to-asset ratio, 18, 126
 deregulation, 22, 27, 39, 60–65
 distrust of, 23
 diversification, 39
 equilibrium, 101
 Glass-Steagall Act repeal and,
  23
 government policies and,
  24–36
 greed and, 24–36
 Greenspan's policies and, 17
 interest rates and, 17–18, 22
 legal action to force subprime
  lending, 47
 nationalization of U.S. banks,
  32–34, 138, 144–146, 149–
  152
 political power, 28–30, 32, 170
 reform, 99–100, 141, 155,
  171–173, 175, 200–201, 216
 resolution procedures, 127,
  132–134, 136–137
 share of U.S. business profits
  1948–2007, 33
 subprime mortgages and, 22
 too-big-to-fail philosophy, 111
 toxic assets, 19, 31, 55–56,
  145, 145n2
 transparency, 102–103, 117,
  133, 141, 195–196, 211
 worker salary increases 1948–
  2007, 33
 See also Community and regional banks; Compensation
  and salaries; Government
  regulation; Mortgage crisis;
  Subprime mortgages; Too-
  big-to-fail banks
BaselineScenario.com, 24
Baucus, Max, 219–223
Bear Stearns
 CEO, 103–104, 200
 collapse, 16, 23
 Federal Reserve and, 117
 government bailout, 169
 hedge funds, 19
 JPMorgan acquisition of, 39,
  77, 131
 size of, 171
Bebchuk, Lucian, 194
Berenson, Alex, 90
Bernanke, Ben
 chairman of Federal Reserve,
  57, 123, 155
 China and, 226, 231
 government mandates for
  Freddie Mac and Fannie
  Mae and, 47, 57
 "Great Moderation" terminol-
  ogy, 199–200
 information capital, 181
 power of, 122
 risk regulation and, 155
 too-big-to-fail banks and,
  122–129
BlackRock, 103
Blair, Tony, 216
Blankfein, Lloyd, 104

Blinder, Alan, 202
Bloomberg, Michael, 103
Bockelmann, Christine, 197
Born, Brooksley, 27, 27n1
Brazil, 232
Bridge banks, 133, 136, 138
Brookings Institution, 89, 224
Brown, Gordon, 216, 220, 232
Buffett, Warren, 92
Buiter, Willem, 144
Bush, George W.
    financial boom and, 27
    housing crisis causes and, 225
    regulation of banking indus-
       try, 48, 51, 60, 61, 63, 65,
       216
    soundness of economy and,
       30–31

C

Cable, Carole, 71
Canada, 70, 72, 74
"Capital infusion", 170
Capital market system, 73
Carlson, Allan C., 134
Carter, Jimmy, 198
Cato Institute, 37, 115, 218
Cato Policy Report, 64
Cayman Islands, 209, 210, 213,
   215, 219
Cayman Islands Monetary Author-
   ity, 218
Cayne, Jimmy, 104, 200
CDOs (collateralized debt
   obligations), 58, 58n9, 210,
   210n7
Center for Universal Education at
   the Council on Foreign Affairs,
   188

Chief executive officers, 81
China
    exports, 68
    financial crisis and, 224–233
    GNP consumption, 68
    Guernsey and, 216
    investment in U.S. bank secu-
       rities, 206
    savings ethic, 206
    Shanghai Composite Index,
       232
    trade imbalances, 225
    U.S. banking crisis and, 26
    U.S. subprime mortgage pur-
       chases, 18
Citigroup, 32, 35, 74, 100, 104,
   170
Clinton, Bill, 27, 50, 62, 97, 188
CNBC, 51
Cohan, William D., 97–105
Collateralized debt obligations
   (CDOs), 58, 58n9, 210, 210n7
Columbia University, 143
Commercial banks, 16, 23, 29, 165
Commodity Futures Moderniza-
   tion Act of 2000, 16
Commodity Futures Trading
   Commission (CFTC), 63, 162
Community and regional banks
    bank crisis solution, 176–187
    financial health, 123
    performance, 177
    role in bank reform, 128–129
    social capital, 178
    solvency, 178
    subprime lending avoidance,
       180
    virtues, 185–187
Community Banking Trust Fund,
   178–179, 183

Community Reinvestment Act
(CRA), 15, 45, 46, 120, 178
Compensation and salaries
banking industry, 66–79
compensation consultants, 198
excessive compensation and
banking crisis, 66–74
golden parachutes, 76, 194–
195
increases, 28
increases 1990–2000, 28
pay caps, 90
performance ties, 191
perverse incentives and, 126
reform, 190–191
responsibility of executives
and, 100
retirement benefits, 194
reward for failure, 195
risk management and, 126,
188–196
"stealth compensation", 194–
195
stock options, 77, 77n3
structure, 191–192
transparency, 195–196
U.S. Congress and, 198
Comptroller of the Currency, 152
Conduits, 210n4
Confucius, 232
Congressional Budget Office Panel
of Economic Advisers, 24
Conservatorship, 38, 136, 145
Construction demand, 17
Consumer Financial Protection
Agency, 171
Continental Illinois National
Bank, 137, 138, 149–152
Controller of the Currency, 64
Cook, Geoff, 214, 215
Corruption, 115, 118

Costa Rica, 213
Council of Economic Advisors, 50,
91
Countrywide Financial, 41
CRA (Community Reinvestment
Act), 15, 45, 46, 120, 178
Credit cards, 113
Credit crisis
international lenders and, 26
investment freeze, 19, 110, 116
spread, 38–39
Credit default swaps
complexity, 103
definition, 16, 27n2, 63n2
government regulation, 63,
162, 162n1
Credit expansion, 41, 85
Credit rating agencies, 23, 73
The Crisis & What to Do About It
(Soros), 14
Cuomo, Andrew M., 192

D

Da Silva, Lula, 232
Daschle, Tom, 222
Debt-to-asset ratio for banks, 18,
126
Defaults, 108
Deflation, 151
Deregulation
banking crisis and, 22, 39,
60–65
banking restructure and, 74
Bush and, 27
Clinton and, 27
definition of, 61n1
See also Government regula-
tion
Derivatives
Chinese purchase, 18

complexity, 103
definition, 16, 162n2, 232n2
Federal Reserve and, 127
government regulation, 162
interest-rate swaps, 27, 27n4
pooling mortgages, 15, 18,
  66–67
too-big-to-fail banks and, 172
value, 85
See also specific types of de-
  rivatives
Dimon, Jamie, 75–79, 104
Disaster recovery, 178
Discrimination in lending, 15
Dodd, Christopher J., 144, 153–
  158
Dorgan, Byron, 219–223
Dow Jones Industrial Average, 120
Down payments on home purchases, 45–46, 53–54, 80
Dunkley, Michael, 216

E

Easy money, 17, 23, 119–121
Economic Recovery Advisory
  Board, 66
Elites, 34, 36
Elliott, Douglas J., 89
Elliott, Francis, 232
Equity funds, 73
Ethics, 146

F

Fahlenbrach, Rüdiger, 199, 200
Farrell, Diana, 171
Federal Deposit Insurance Company (FDIC)
  bank regulation and, 161–162
  chairpersons, 149, 169

community banks and, 177
Continental Illinois Bank and,
  150
intervention and resolution
  process, 32–34, 112, 117,
  155, 169
nationalization of U.S. banks
  and, 152
risk regulation, 155
rule changes, 64
too-big-to-fail banks and, 165,
  167, 174
Federal Home Loan Mortgage
  Corporation (Freddie Mac)
  affordable housing goals, 47
  bank insolvencies and, 117
  banking crisis responsibility,
    26
  bankruptcy, 38, 41, 82
  corruption, 120
  CRA ratings, 46–47
  creation of, 14
  government conservatorship,
    38, 169
  guarantor of mortgages, 15,
    45
  housing bubble factor, 48–49
  leverage, 83
  mortgage-backed security in-
    vestments, 57, 108
  political contributions and,
    118
  pooling mortgages, 15
  U.S. Treasury and, 48
Federal Housing Administration
  (FHA), 45
Federal National Mortgage Association (Fannie Mae)
  affordable housing goals, 47
  banking crisis responsibility,
    26
  bankruptcy, 38, 41, 82

corruption, 120
creation of, 14
government conservatorship, 38, 145, 169
guarantor of mortgages, 15, 45
housing bubble factor, 48–49
leverage, 83
mortgage-backed security investments, 57, 108
political contributions and, 118
pooling mortgages, 15
U.S. Treasury and, 48
Federal Reserve
adjustable rate Mortgages and, 42–43
central bank of U.S., 70
credit expansion policy, 41
deregulation of banking industry, 64
derivative markets and, 127
easy money policy, 17, 23, 119–121
housing bubble creation, 48–49
interest rates, 16–17, 42, 110
money supply, 42
nationalization of U.S. banks and, 144, 152
power, 155, 175
rates and inflation targets 1999–2008, 44
regulation of banks, 163, 171–172
response to recession, 16
See also specific chairpersons
Federal Reserve Bank of Kansas City, 130
Fernholz, Tim, 168–175
Financial Accounting Standards Board, 102

Financial engineering, 68–70
Financial Services Committee, 170
Financial Services Modernization Act of 1999, 39
Financial Stability Board, 214
Financial Stability Forum, 193–194
Financial Times (newspaper), 207, 226
"Flipping" properties, 40
Foreclosures, 19, 38, 56, 84
Foreign tax havens
arbitrage and, 215, 215n10
Bahamas, 210, 216
banking crisis contribution, 218–223
banking secrecy, 211
Cayman Islands, 209, 213, 215
collateralized debt obligations (CDOs), 210, 210n7
Guernsey, 211
information-sharing agreements, 213
"offshore" wealth, 209
shadow banking, 210
structured investment vehicles, 210
Switzerland, 209, 212–214
tax evasion, 212–213
tax rates, 209
U.S. tax gap and, 215
401(k) plans, 28
France, 117
Frank, Barney, 79, 198, 202
Fraud, 213
Free University of Berlin, 207
Fried, Jesse, 194
Fuld, Richard, 103, 104, 200
Futures industry, 162, 162n3

G

G20, 213–214, 213n9, 220–221, 220n1

Gambling, 216

Garvey, John, 89

Gattuso, James L., 60–65

Geithner, Tim
    executive compensation and, 189–190
    Federal Reserve as bank regulator, 163
    offshore investments, 222
    shadow banking and, 210
    too-big-to-fail banks and, 169–170
    Wachovia Bank failure and, 175

General Motors, 28

Germany, 117

Glass-Steagall Act repeal, 23, 165, 167

Global governance, 229

GNP (gross national product), 67–68

Gold standard, 231

Golden parachute, 76, 76n2

Goldman Sachs, 39, 49, 102, 104

"Good Bank," 145

Gota Bank (Sweden), 152

Government Accountability Office, 63, 213

Government regulation
    avoidance, 161
    bank blockage of, 160
    banking crisis and, 27, 52–59, 111
    banking industry reform and, 73, 154
    banking regulation reform, 141, 171, 173, 175
    bifurcated banking system and, 73
    business conduct and, 156
    complexity, 78
    derivatives, 16
    Federal Reserve, 163, 171, 173
    financial stability and, 156
    government support of banking institutions and, 72, 111
    GSEs (government-sponsored enterprises), 48, 48n7
    leverage excesses, 85–86
    objectives, 156
    regulator judgment, 159, 174
    repeal, 29
    "safety and soundness" regulation, 160
    subprime mortgage lending and, 22, 41, 43, 45–48
    super regulator, 162

Grading agencies, 69

Gramm-Leach-Bliley Act, 39, 62–63

Great Depression, 36, 67, 89, 92, 118, 141

"Great Moderation", 199–200

Greed, 24–36, 39, 209

Greenberg, Hank, 104

Greenspan, Alan
    criticism of Freddie Mac and Fannie Mae and, 57
    deregulation and, 163
    money supply expansion, 42, 43
    responsibility for banking crisis, 17, 30–31

Gregory, David, 91–96

Gross domestic product (GDP), 226

Gross national product (GNP), 67–68, 85, 93, 113

Group of 30, 70, 70n2

GSEs (government-sponsored enterprises), 48, 48n7

Guardian (UK newspaper), 142

Guernsey, 211, 216

Guernsey Finance, 214

Guerrera, Francesco, 78

Gutierrez, Luis, 181

H

Hanke, Steve, 42

Health care, 109, 110

Hedge funds
    asset disposal, 147
    Bear Stearns hedge funds, 19, 30n9
    conflicts of interest, 73
    definition of, 73n3, 100n1, 210n3
    foreign tax havens, 210
    housing and finance bubbles and, 30
    interest rate swaps, 27n4
    profits, 211

Henderson, David R., 64

Heritage Foundation, 60, 115, 201

Hispanic Americans, 54

Hoenig, Thomas M., 130–138

Home ownership rates, 17

Hoover, Herbert, 118

Housing bubble
    arbitrage and, 68–69
    bust, 22, 23, 108, 120
    factors creating, 17, 42–43, 48–49, 116
    housing cycle, 81
    housing prices, 18–19, 80
    See also Real estate

I

Iceland, 232

Income. *See* Compensation and salaries

Information capital, 181

Information-sharing agreements, 213

Institute for Global Economic Growth, 218

Interest only mortgages, 53

Interest-rate swaps, 27, 27n4

Interest rates
    banking crisis cause, 17–18, 22, 26
    easy money, 23
    Federal Reserve lowering, 16–17, 109
    interest-rate swaps, 27, 27n4
    volatility, 27

Internal Revenue Service (IRS), 211–213

International Monetary Fund
    chief economist, 24, 165
    clients, 25
    global governance, 229
    political power of U.S. banking industry and, 29
    response to U.S. banking crisis, 32, 34–35
    responsibility for U.S. housing bubble and, 43

Investment banking. *See* Banking industry

IRA, 28

Isaac, William M., 149–152

It's a Wonderful Life (film), 14, 134, 181, 187

J

Jacobson, Beth, 56
Japan, 35, 116–118
Jefferson, Thomas, 104
Jersey, 216
Jersey Finance, 214
Job creation, 109
Johnson, Simon, 24–36, 33, 165
JPMorgan Chase & Co.
    Bear Stearns acquired by, 19,
        39, 77, 77n4, 131
    CEO, 103–104
    compensation packages, 75,
        76, 78
    deregulation and, 39
    toxic assets, 103
    Washington Mutual acquired
        by, 77n4
Junk bonds, definition, 40n4
Junk mortgages, 40, 41, 41n5
    See also Subprime mortgages

K

Keeler, Rachel, 208–217
Keynes, John Maynard, 121
"Keynesian beauty contest", 121
Kubarych, Roger M., 172
Kudlow, Larry, 51

L

Lacker, Jeffrey, 141
Laissez-faire capitalism, 53, 532
Landler, Mark, 207
Lawsuits, 82
Lehman Brothers
    bankruptcy, 89, 101
    CEO, 103, 104, 200
    collapse, 16, 23, 26, 41, 49, 82,
        89
    credit freeze and, 26
    Federal Reserve and, 117
    global effect of bankruptcy,
        11, 146
    size, 171
    stock price, 89
    subprime mortgage invest-
        ments, 89
Leverage
    community and regional
        banks, 183
    definition, 81n1, 184n4, 210n2
    executive compensation and,
        risk, 189
    maximum leverage, 82–83
    no leverage, 82
    partial leverage, 82
    rate of return, 82–83
Levin, Carl, 212, 219–223
Levitt, Arthur, 170–171
Lewis, Kenneth D., 104, 151, 167
Lewis, Sandy B., 97–105
Liar loans, 53
Liechtenstein, 213
Liquidity, 144, 144n1
Liquidity management, 126
Lobbyists, 211
London School of Economics, 144
Longman, Phillip, 176–187
Low-income borrowers, 46
Lucas, Robert, 222
Lula da Silva, Luiz Inacio, 232
Luxembourg, 213

M

M2 money supply, 42, 42n6
MacIntosh, Julie, 78
Mack, John, 104
Madoff, Bernard, 221, 222
Malaysia, 26, 213

Martin, William McChesney, 16–17, 193

Maryland, 56

Mason, David M., 201

Massachusetts Institute of Technology Sloan School of Management, 24, 166

Maximum leverage, 82–83

McCain, John, 91–94

McCaskill, Claire, 212

Meet the Press (TV show), 91

Mergers and acquisitions
Bank of America acquisition of Merril Lynch & Co., 20, 39, 62, 167
risk managements, 16
too-big-to-fail banks, 166

Merrill Lynch & Co.
Bank of America acquisition of, 20, 39, 62, 167
CEO, 104, 200
collapse, 19, 41, 49, 82

Minorities, 54, 56

Mitchell, Daniel, 115–121

Monetary Economics Projects of the National Bureau of Economic Research, 122

Morgan, J.P., 28

Morgan Stanley, 39, 49, 102, 104

Morris, Charles R., 85

Mortgage
balloon mortgages, 15
foreclosures, 19, 38, 56, 84
interest only mortgages, 53
legislation concerning, 15
negative amortization mortgages, 15, 53, 534
pooling mortgages, 15, 18, 66–67

See also Adjustable rate mortgages (ARMs); Subprime mortgages

Mortgage-backed securities
cash flow reductions and, 40
definition, 38n1, 57n8, 81n2
leverage excesses, 81–84
pooling mortgages, 15, 18, 66–67, 107
price decline, 38, 40
toxic securities, 55–56

Mortgage crisis
banking crisis and, 22
banking regulation failures, 52–59
China and, 224–229
CRA loan defaults, 46–47
default risks of subprime mortgages, 40
definition of subprime mortgage, 52n1
definition of subprime mortgage crisis, 231n1
down payments, 45–47, 53–54, 80
excessive debt as cause, 80–86
Federal Reserve interest rates and, 17–18
foreclosures, 19, 38, 56, 84
foreign investment, 206
foreign tax havens, 208–217
government policies and, 15, 22–23, 41, 43, 45–48
leverage excesses, 81–84
NINJA loans, 18, 53, 53n3, 54
pooling mortgages, 18
predatory lending, 52, 54–55, 181–182
taxpayer subsidization, 45

See also Bailouts; Banking industry; Subprime mortgages

N

National Bureau of Economic Research, 224
National Recovery Administration New Deal, 64
Nationalization, definition, 145n3
Nationalization of U.S. banks, 32–34, 138, 144–146, 149–152
Negative amortization mortgages, 15, 53, 534
Nelson, Bill, 212
New America Foundation, 176
New Deal, 64
New York Federal Reserve, 75, 169
New York Stock Exchange, 102
New York Times (newspaper), 32, 90, 197, 207
Nikkei, 116
NINJA loans, 18, 53, 53n3, 54
Niven, Peter, 214
Nixon, Richard, 120–121, 231
No leverage, 82
Nobel Prize, 142, 143, 222
Nonprime mortgages, definition, 40n3
    See also Subprime mortgages
Norris, Floyd, 197–203
Northern Illinois University College of Business, 22
Norway, 144

O

Obama, Barack
    bailouts and, 106–114
    banking system reform, 141, 171, 200–201, 216
    breakup of too-big-to-fail banks, 165
    China and, 226
    Congress and, 154
    criticism of, 218
    criticism of McCain, 93, 94
    economic policies, 34, 91, 92–96, 98–99, 101, 160
    election, 105
    foreign tax havens and, 212
    lack of transparency in financial markets and, 102–103
    nationalization of banks and, 152
    "perfect storm" crisis metaphor and, 22
    regulation of banking system, 61, 90
    too-big-to-fail banks and, 111
OECD (Organization for Economic Development), 213, 221
Offshore financial centers (OFCs), 221
Offshore tax havens. *See* Foreign tax havens
Ohio State University, 199
Oil exporting countries, 227
Old Bank, 145
Oligarchy, 30, 30n8
Oligopoly, 72
OMX Index (Iceland), 232
O'Neal, Stan, 104, 200
Organization for Economic Development (OECD), 213, 221

P

Partial leverage, 82
Patient capital, 178
Paulson, Henry, 31, 32, 104, 206, 231
Pauly, David, 164–167
Pearlstein, Steven, 159–163
Pelosi, Nancy, 61

Personal debt, 16, 30

Peterson Institute for International Economics, 24

Pew Research Center, 111

Philippines, 213

Ponzi scheme, 222

Pooling mortgages, 15, 18, 66–67, 107

Powell, Michael, 56

Prasad, Eswar, 224–229

Predatory lending, 52, 54–55, 181–182

Price controls, 120–121

PricewaterhouseCoopers, 89

Princeton University, 202

Private equity firms, definition of, 100n2, 210n4

Private mortgage insurance, 45–46

Procyclical system, 124, 124n1, 128

Progressive Era, 187

Protectionism, 118

Public Private Investment Program, 99

Putin, Vladimir, 22

R

Rahn, Richard W., 218–223

Rangel, Charles, 222

Rate of return, 82–83

Reagan, Ronald, 27

Real estate
down payments, 45–47
hedge funds and, 73n3
home ownership rates, 17
housing price declines, 18–19
Japanese real estate market, 117–118
prices, 17, 108

See also Housing bubble; Mortgage

Recessions, 52–53, 67, 107, 121, 164, 200

Reconstruction Finance Corporation (RFC), 130, 138

Red River Valley Regional Bank, 167

Regional banks. *See* Community and regional banks

Regulation. *see* Government regulation

Regulation Q, 185–186

Reid, Harry, 99

Resolution procedures, 127, 132–134, 136–137

RGE Monitor, 50

Richmond (Virginia) Federal Reserve, 141

Risk management
adjustable-rate mortgages, 43
bailouts and, 119
bank reform, 99–100, 155, 171–173
community banks, 129–130, 183
derivatives, 16
execessive credit and, 85
executive compensation and, 66–74, 76, 188–196
Fannie Mae and Freddie Mac and, 57
financial crisis and, 81, 84
government mandates and, 43–49
incentives, 141
legislation, 181
mergers and acquisitions, 16
regulation and measurement of, 30, 62, 126–127, 155–157, 162–163

subprime mortgage invest-
ments, 17–18, 40–41, 107–
108
"tail risk", 192
too-big-to-fail banks and, 16,
124–126, 133, 171–173
transparency and, 117
Ritholtz, Barry, 22
Roberts, Russell, 47
Romer, Christina, 91–96
Roosevelt, Franklin Delano, 14, 34,
64, 118
Roosevelt, Theodore, 34–35
Rose, Charlie, 98
Roubini, Nouriel, 50–59
Rubin, Robert, 22, 63, 104
Russia, 26

S

Salaries. *See* Compensation and
salaries
Salary increase, 28
Sarbanes-Oxley Act, 76, 76n1, 202
Sarkozy, Nicolas, 214, 220
Savings, 206
Savingtoinvest.com, 80
S.B. Lewis & Company, 97
Schularick, Moritz, 207, 226
Schwartz, Alan, 103–104
The Secura Group, 149
Securities, definition, 73n5, 78n5,
107n1
Securities and Exchange Commission
absence of enforcement, 29
bank leverage regulation, 18,
23
banking industry debt-to-asset
ratio and, 18, 23
chairpersons, 170
hedge fund regulation, 215
investor protection, 162
Lewis and, 97
rulemaking activities, 63
short selling securities and,
151–152
transparency in banking and,
103
Securitization
creation of concept, 14–15, 27
definition, 27n3, 57n7
Freddie Mac and Fannie Mae
and, 57
Lehman Brothers, 200, 200n1
pooling mortgages and, 15
Seeking Alpha, 80
Seidman, Ellen, 176–187
Shadow banking, 210, 210n1
Shanghai Composite Index
(China), 232
Shorebank Corporation, 176
Short selling stocks, 151
Simpson, Marc, 22
Social capital, 178
Soros, George, 14, 101, 145, 211
South Korea, 26
"Special affordable" loans, 47
Sperling, Gene, 188–196
"Stealth compensation", 194–195
Stern School of Business, New
York University, 50
Stiglitz, Joseph, 142, 143–148
Stock market bubble, 68
Stock options, 77, 77n3
"Stress test" of banking by U.S.
Treasury, 36, 90, 99, 110, 170
Structured investment vehicles,
210, 210n6
Stulz, René, 199, 200, 201

Subprime mortgages
default risks of subprime
mortgages, 40
defaults, 108
definition, 52n1, 180n3, 190n2
down payments, 45–47, 53–
54, 80
executive compensation and
growth of, 190
government mandate, 22, 41,
43, 45–48
junk mortgages, 40, 41, 41n5
Lehman Brothers and, 89
NINJA loans, 18, 53, 53n3, 54
See also Mortgage; Mortgage-
backed securities; Mortgage
crisis
Sweden, 130, 137, 138, 144, 152
Swiss Federal Institute of Technology, 199
Switzerland, 209, 212–214, 219

T

"Tail risk", 192
TARP (Troubled Asset Relief
Program), 76, 90, 104, 110, 183
Tax evasion, 212–213, 219
Tax information exchange, 219
Tax Justice Network, 209
Tax Notes, 209
Tax protectionism, 219
Tax rate increases, 118
Tax Reform Act of 1986, 15
Term Asset-Backed Securities Loan
Facility, 99
Terrorist attacks of September 11,
16
Think tanks, 60, 176, 218, 224
Thomas A. Roe Institute for Eco-
nomic Policy Studies, 60

Time (magazine), 75
Tokyo Stock Exchange, 116
Too-big-to-fail banks
allowance for failure of, 130–
138
asset statistics, 135
bailout effect, 163
Bernanke on, 122–129
breakup recommendations,
150–151, 164–167
compensation of executives,
142
conservatorship and, 136
Continental Illinois Bank
comparison, 151–152
control of banking industry,
182–183
criticism of system, 156
effect of failures, 146
equity of treatment, 133
free market system allowance
for failure of, 130–138
Obama and, 111
prevention of formation of,
156
recklessness, 164
resolution procedures, 127,
132–134, 136–137
risk management, 124–126
role, 172
unfairness of government
bailouts, 170
See also Banking industry
Tourism, 216
Toxic assets, 19, 31, 55–56, 145,
145n2
Tranches, definition, 18
Transparency, 102–103, 117, 133,
141, 195–196

U

UBS Bank, 211
Ugland House (Cayman Islands), 213
Unemployment, 108, 109, 209
United Kingdom (UK), 70, 73
University of California, Berkeley, 91
University of Cambridge, 207
University of Missouri–St. Louis, 37
U.S. Congress, 38, 48, 90, 104
   See also specific committees
U.S. Department of Housing and Urban Development (HUD), 38, 47, 48–49
U.S. Department of Treasury
   bailout of Bank of America, 32
   bank ownership, 184–185
   Fannie Mae and Freddie Mac backing, 48
   regulation of off-shore business, 219–223
   secretaries, 18, 31, 32, 57, 63, 104
   "stress test", 36, 90, 99, 110, 170
The U.S. Financial and Economic Crisis: Where Does It Stand and Where Do We Go from Here (Baily and Elliott), 89

U.S. House of Representatives Financial Services Committee, 77, 191, 201–203
U.S. Senate Banking, Housing, and Urban Affairs Committee, 153, 154
U.S. Senate Finance Committee, 220
U.S. Treasury bonds, 228
USA Today (newspaper), 89

V

Volcker, Paul, 27, 66–74

W

Wachovia Bank, 117, 157, 169, 175
Wage controls, 120–121
Wall Street Journal (WSJ; newspaper), 52, 151, 202
Washington Mutual, 77, 117
Weill, Sanford, 104
Wells Fargo Bank, 56
Wen Jiabao, 206
White, Lawrence H., 37–49
Whitehouse, Sheldon, 212
Wilson, Garff B., 91
Wolin, Neal, 173–174

X

Xinhua News Agency, 230–233